HARVEY CARIG
KILL___

PETE DOVE

Out of Control – The Story of Harvey Carignan

From the side angle of his most recent mugshot, Harvey the Hammer (surely, not one of the better nicknames to be hung on the shoulders of a serial killer) still looks like the murderer he is. Flat of nose, shaven headed, protruding chin on his jowly, hanging face, this now old man still retains the features of a childhood nightmare.

But from front on, we see his eyes. They are overhung by flabby eyebrows, and sitting deep inside their sockets, seem dark and broody. There is a half-smile on his face. Not a smirk, not a smile of smugness, but a smile of acquiescence. The face lacks symmetry. One eye sits higher than the other, the nose is twisted to one side, no doubt the result of one or more of the many fracas that have littered his life. The lines dripping from his nose are of different lengths, the wobbling flesh they hold back a dull, dusky pink.

But it is the eyes which call you. Another of the monikers attached to this vicious rapist and killer is the 'Want Ad Murderer', because he would sometimes find his victims through ads placed in the local press. They are eyes full of want. Not desire, note, but need. From this front on view Harvey Carignan changes. He is the cuddly great grandfather who would envelope our kids in hugs and slobbery kisses. He is the man who knows he has little time left and is scared by that thought. Maybe even a man with regrets. We might feel for him. Almost.

Then again, perhaps we know more than those sad eyes tell us. Perhaps we know the real Harvey Carignan. A man who murdered at least five victims. Whose convictions are for attempted murder as well as murder itself, for assault, attempted rape, burglary, and sodomy. Can we still hold the slightest empathy for this man? Would doing so betray the memory of his victims, now long dead?

It is hard to say. For humans. Not, though, for the American justice system, which last turned down his attempt to gain parole in 2015, when Carignan was eighty-eight years old, and surely too frail to be a

Harvey Carignan, Serial Killer

Pete Dove

Published by Trellis Publishing, 2021.

HARVEY CARIGNAN, SERIAL KILLER

First edition. July 4, 2021.

Copyright © 2021 Pete Dove.

ISBN: 979-8224165186

Written by Pete Dove.

threat anymore. Were they right? Let us take a look at his case, and judge for ourselves.

Carignan was not – maybe is still not – of the soundest mind. That despite his faux interest in psychology that he has built up during his lonely hours locked away. He referred to himself as 'An instrument of God, one who was acting under His personal instructions. Murder, rape, and mutilation are all part of a Grand Plan. God is a figure with a large hood, and you can't see his face.' This habit of referring to himself in the third person could easily be viewed as an attempt to shift guilt away from himself; shift it on to God, or on to this remote self. Perhaps to excuse guilt from his soul in any form at all.

Certainly, it was his excuse when caught, for a murder spree that included at least five women, and possibly up to eighteen. When looked at in the context of other crimes he committed, it does not stand up to even a passing scrutiny. Let us be clear. Harvey Carignan was either evil, or mad. Maybe he remains so today, and that explains the parole board's unwillingness to consider his case.

He was born in 1927. May 18th was the day the world began to carry his burden. (Although, maybe not. Carignan himself is unsure of the exact date of his birth. Still, as he says, 'it doesn't make a hell of a lot of difference at this time in my life.') The small city of Fargo, in North Dakota was his home for his early years. Although unsurprisingly his birth does not appear among the details of the city's alumni, he is still possibly the most famous thing to come from this unremarkable place. The city was named after a director of the Northern Pacific Railroad, William G Fargo. It was a tough place. A frontier town filled with saloons and bordellos, its population of just 600 swelled by itinerant workers drawn by the new railroad.

Fargo was founded in 1871, but within twenty years had grown to a reasonable size – 8000 settlers were now drawn by its promise of cheap farming land, ground which was fertile enough to offer some return for any prepared to work hard. Wood framed buildings begin to replace the temporary tents which marked its initial days. A major fire swept through these wooden homes in 1893, destroying much of the fledgling city. They were replaced within a year, now with more substantial structures many of which still remain today. Despite attempts from the city board to attract visitors today there is not much more to say. Yes, a fine bridge marks one end of the city, but it is still a relatively poor place. Indeed, many would argue that the most significant event to take place between the fire of 1893 and the present day was the birth of a particular child in, probably, 1927.

Carignan's early years were unimaginably tough. If he did indeed suffer from mental illness, it is not hard to trace its roots. If he was evil, again it is easy to see the most likely place from which that state emerged. His mother was just twenty, and unmarried, when she gave birth to a child who would become a monster. Few details remain regarding the woman, although we know that she did finally marry, by which time Harvey was three or four, and she had a second son who was much more the family favourite. Perhaps, not least, because she knew the name of his dad.

The next information we have about young Harvey comes when he is six. It is 1933 and America is in the grips of the Great Depression. Harvey is not faring well. He is undersized and has a twitch which afflicts his face. Much is made of the facts that we also know he was a habitual bed wetter, and also enjoyed the company of a special friend called Paul. This friend was, though, imaginary. Certainly, many young children wet the bed, and many more become close to imaginary friends. However, given what happened later, we might conclude that Harvey was a child suffering. We do not know the details of this suffering – neglect, abuse, witness to domestic abuse – we can only surmise. However, by the age of eight it seems as though his biological mother had endured enough, and he was sent to live with his aunt and uncle. This was in Cavalier, North Dakota, one hundred and sixty miles to the south. He may as well have been banished to another country.

Any hope that the boy might receive love and care in the bosom of his aunt was short-lived. Within months he was back home and subject to the dubious attentions of his mother and, we believe, his stepfather. By ten he was still bed wetting daily, and was farmed out once more, this time to his grandmother. Now the full width of the state was positioned between mother and son. Perhaps it is not surprising that the boy made no progress there (not least, perhaps, because this grandmother's own record at bringing up children was hardly exemplary). He was soon on the move again, to another aunt and then back to his mother. From there, institutionalisation beckoned, and he found himself in reform school.

It is impossible to understate just how disruptive a lifestyle such as this must be to any child, let alone one suffering clear developmental issues. Feeling so abandoned at such a vulnerable age must surely have aggravated his lack of self-esteem, no doubt already heightened by his bed wetting into early adolescence. Finally, Harvey did receive a diagnosis of sorts. Doctors decided that he was suffering from a neurological condition called Chorea. This unpleasant illness is named in somewhat bad taste after the Greek word for dancing because children with this condition twitch purposelessly and uncontrollably, suffering sessions when at rest and when sleeping.

The condition is also associated with depression, lack of concentration and behavioural disorders. It would certainly have added to the difficulties Harvey experienced when socialising with adults or peers. It is certainly not surprising given the lack of stability in his life that by the time he was eleven, he was stealing regularly, and thus ended up in reform school. It did not help his overall sense of self-worth that, according to his own accounts, he was subjected to sexual abuse by female staff when in there. His reports of this were, though, never substantiated.

As soon as he was old enough, aged eighteen, Carignan joined the US army. It was while he was serving here, in Alaska, that he committed the first murder for which he was charged (whether he was already a killer by this point, we do not know for certain). Laura Showatler was fifty-seven years old and died as a result of numerous blows to the head. She had also been raped.

Within a couple of months of committing this crime, Carignan was at it again. His victim this time was called Dorcas Callen. She managed to escape and reported to police that she had been approached by a drunk soldier at seven o clock in the morning. He had pressured her and attempted to rape her, but she had escaped.

Police arranged an identity line up and both Dorcas and an eyewitness to the attack, John Keith, named Carignan as the culprit. It was the start of a rapid downturn, if such a thing were possible, in the young soldier's fortune. US Marshalls became involved and questioned the man about the murder of Laura Showatler.

Apparently, he confessed. But only orally. There was no written confession ever made. But Harvey was a 'bad one'; in reform school from age eleven, stealing before his teens, abandoned by his parents and so on. There was strong evidence that he had attempted to rape another woman. In the post war boom the US was enjoying there was no place for such an outsider, and whether or not Carignan had indeed killed Laura, he was tried and easily convicted. In 1950 it seemed as though his short and unhappy time on earth was coming to a premature end. He was sentenced to death by hanging.

But that confession caused concerns in many quarters. Had it been genuinely obtained? Was it a true and proper confession? Or had Harvey made his statement because an officer keen to settle the case had promised he would avoid the death penalty if he admitted the crime? Had he indeed made such a confession? His lawyers thought not, and within a year his case was up before the Supreme Court, who ruled that the death sentence be voided. This appeal rested on the McNabb Mallory rule, which states that confessions must not be used in evidence if they are obtained when an unreasonably long period has passed between arrest and court appearance.

Nevertheless, the Supreme Court were still aware of the rape conviction against Dorcas, and he did not get away lightly. He was moved to the notorious Alcatraz prison, where he spent another eight years before being paroled in April 1960. He did not remain a free man for long. Within four months he had committed crimes of assault, attempted rape, and burglary. This time in Minnesota, and he was sentenced to two and a half years there, and another spell totalling more than six years for offences in Kansas. It is often said that prisons are breeding places for criminal behaviour. That certainly seemed to be the case with Carignan. He was released in under four years, and within six months was back inside once more. This time for burglary, committed in Washington State, where the authorities clearly seemed to have had enough of this one-man crime wave. He was sentenced to fifteen years in the notorious Walla Wall penitentiary.

But Carignan must have had some element of charm about him. Whilst inside he appeared to try to make something of himself, completing his High School Diploma and trying out some college courses. Less than four years into his fifteen-year stint he was paroled once more. Life, for a very short time, appeared to improve. Back on the outside he married – his wife (or perhaps 'victim' is a better term) was one Sheila Moran. The poor woman and her daughter soon discovered that the man about the house remained one keen to be about other people's houses. Once more Carignan was arrested, and sent back to Walla Walla, this time for the combination of robbery and parole violation. He was never charged for the physical abuse he laid on Sheila, but she took the opportunity of his time in custody to launch a divorce claim for physical abuse. They had been together for less than a year.

Another factor in her need to get away from her new husband was his strange behaviour. Carignan was depressive, there is no doubt about that. Maybe Sheila could have lived with this if his sullen moods had not manifested themselves in violence and a strange need to get up in the middle of the night and drive for hours. His excuse that he 'needed to be alone and think' may have been true, but given that he refused to explain about what it was he was thinking, or where he was travelling to have these thoughts, Sheila became suspicious. Looking back, we can only speculate about what it was he was doing on those long drives. That some criminal behaviour was involved is a consideration which cannot be ignored.

For three years little was heard of from Carignan. Which is not to say that he was not active in a criminal sense. Indeed, it seems more than likely that his offending had returned to its highest forms of violence which he had, probably, inflicted on his victims back in Alaska during his army days.

However, he stayed off the radar of the authorities. Any hope that he had turned a corner in his life was, though, forlorn. On April 14th, 1972 he married for a second time, another divorcee with children of her own. The unfortunate woman was Alice Johnson, and the even more innocent victims were her son and daughter, Billy – who was eleven at the time – and his fourteen-year-old sister Georgia. Within two months of this man setting foot inside the family home, Billy was off to live with his real dad. He could no longer cope with the physical beatings laid on him by his new, presumably unwanted, stepfather.

It is interesting, in a cold and calculating way, that it was Billy who bore the brunt of Carignan's domestic violence. Was this in some way Harvey enacting the own abuse he suffered as a child? Or, was he unable to accept that a boy might be happy, and loved, within a family home? There is no doubt that Carignan was – is perhaps – a very, very bad man. The extent to which this stemmed from the abusive childhood he endured cannot be overstated.

Whether marriage turned his head, or whether he was already undertaking large scale serial killings, is something of which we cannot be absolutely sure. Giving him the benefit of a considerable doubt, there is no question that Carignan entered the most destructive phase of his already violence filled life. He was forty-five years old, beginning to bald, and perhaps believed that marriage gave him a gravitas to protect him against the crimes he was about to commit. Who knows? Harvey Carignan was not the most spectacular firework in the box when it came to brains. Even if he was among the deadliest when let off without careful supervision.

He had been married only just a little over three months when Virginia Piper disappeared. The wife of a wealthy CEO was released after payment of a million-dollar ransom. Whilst the alleged perpetrators were caught, their convictions were later squashed. Some speculate that she could have been a victim of Carignan's. It seems unlikely, given that he was neither seen to suddenly splash around plenty of money, nor was it likely that he had the intelligence to plan such an audacious kidnapping, in broad daylight on a sumptuous estate. However, when Leslie Laura Brock, a nineteen-year-old from Bellingham, Washington, was found dead in October of the same year, Carignan seemed a likely culprit. The manner of her death fitted his modus operandi, she was hit several times over the head with what was probably a claw hammer. Later, a witness claimed to have seen her getting into a truck similar to the one Carignan owned. Meanwhile, his stepdaughter Georgia, just fifteen by now, was struggling to cope with the sickening advances Carignan was making towards her. In the end, she could live there no longer, and ran away. Within another six to eight months, Alice decided to leave her abusive husband. He was arrested for assaulting her in early July 1973 and enough was enough.

Between the death of Laura Brock and the final attack on his wife, two other women went missing, one no more than a girl. Kathy Sue Miller was a teenager – just fifteen years old – looking to earn some pocket money from working a part time job. She had answered an advertisement in a local paper seeking an assistant to work in a service station. The man who was leasing the station was Harvey Carignan, and when Kathy showed up to be interviewed, he sexually abused and killed the terrified young girl. Her body, naked and wrapped carelessly in a sheet of plastic, was not found until several months later. Two boys had been hiking in a reserve near Everett, Washington, when they made their gruesome discovery. Kathy's head with peppered by holes. They had been made with blows from a claw hammer.

Kathy's death was on May 1st, 1973. On June 28th Mary Townsend was waiting for a bus when she was attacked from behind and knocked unconscious. She woke to discover herself in a vehicle with a man approaching middle age who demanded sex. Mary was older – 47 – and more worldly than Kathy and managed to leap from the vehicle. Although she had seen her attacker clearly, he remained at large.

Jerri Billings was only thirteen years old when she made the foolish decision to hitch a lift; the driver who stopped was no knight in a shining silver van, but Carignan. He forced the child to perform sex acts on him and then began to beat her with the hammer. Something, though, caused him to stop before he killed his young victim, and he released her. Terrified, she ran home but did not reveal the cause of her injuries or the details of her ordeal until many months later.

Still the attacks continued. Carignan was like a man possessed. The Jerri Billings' attack took place in September 1973. A year later, in August 1974 Ellen Hunley disappeared. What is remarkable here is that Hunley was Carignan's ex-girlfriend. He had picked her up as she hitchhiked in Minnesota, which was to where Carignan had moved, and the two had started a relationship. Inevitably, it could not last and after a couple of months Hunley broke it off. When her body was discovered in September 1974, it was found that Ellen had, like several victims before, been killed with blows from an instrument which matched the description of a hammer. Alarmingly, this victim had been sexually violated with a tree branch. Carignan really was a very depraved man.

By September 1974 Carignan's offending was totally out of control. So much so that it is hard to reason that he was anything but insane during this period at the very least.

On September 8th he picked up two more hitchhikers who were travelling in Minneapolis. He drove them out of town, he stopped the vehicle and began beating seventeen-year-old June Lynch with a hammer. Meanwhile, her sixteen-year-old friend, Lisa King, managed to escape and ran off screaming for help. Carignan bundled June out of his vehicle and sped away.

Six days later Carignan picked up another young woman, Gwen Burton, from a parking lot. He choked her, assaulted her, and struck her with a hammer before leaving her by the roadside, assuming that she was dead. But Carignan was careless killer, and Gwen survived, managing to attract the attention of another driver.

On the 18th of the month he picked up two more teenaged hitchhikers, Sally Versoi and Dianne Flynn. He forced them to take it in turns to perform oral sex on him, using the hammer to coerce them into performing his perverted wishes. But once again, he demonstrated his inability to commit his crimes with any degree of competence. He stopped for gas, and both girls managed to escape.

Kathy Shultz was less lucky. The student failed to turn up at her school on the 20th September. Her body was found the following day in a cornfield forty miles from Minneapolis. She had not survived, murdered with savage blows from a hammer.

Did Carignan plan his crimes? Did he go out looking for victims? Were his crimes driven by an insatiable sexual appetite? Were the number of victims who managed to escape down to a wish on his part, once the sex was over, down to the fact that he did feel guilt for what he had done? Was he simply insane? His mind warped by his childhood horrors, the abuse, violence and, possibly, sexual molestation to which he fell victim in his early years coming home to roost?

Again, we cannot be sure. The US Criminal Justice System of the 1970s, like those in other parts of the world, held little interest in either rehabilitation or in understanding the reasons for criminal behaviour. A shame because Carignan could have made a very interesting case study.

However, the police could not fail to see the pattern in the crimes taking place under their noses. Finally, officers in Minneapolis began to talk to investigators dealing with similar cases in Washington State. Carignan's identity began to come up, and victims of abduction began to pick his features from line ups.

Matters became even more frightening. A search of his home revealed a number of maps marked with red circles. One hundred and eighty-one of these. The circles related to three things. Where he had applied for jobs (he was working on a construction site by now), where he had purchased vehicles, and where women had been the victim of unsolved homicides and assaults. The circles stretched north into Canada.

Minnesotan law states that no criminal can be sentenced to more than forty years in prison. Carignan was tried in February 1975 for the attempted murder and aggravated sodomy of Gwen Burton. He and his lawyers attempted, perhaps reasonably enough, to claim insanity as a mitigating circumstance. Joseph Friedberg, his defence attorney forty five years ago, argued that his client believed God had instructed him to 'degrade and kill certain women,' and that 'Harvey Carignan believes to this day as he sits here before you that he has failed the Lord. He deliberately attempted to kill that young lady (Gwen, who was, incidentally, a student nurse – a highly reputably profession) and he blames where he is right now on the fact that a woman would not die.'

The jury did not buy the defence's argument and found him guilty. He was sentenced to the maximum forty-year term, with other sentences of thirty years for assaulting Jerri Billings, and forty for the murders of both Eileen Hunley and Kathy Schultz given at further trials. He should have been released in 2015, having served his forty years. But Carignan remains behind bars.

Harvey Carignan will be 95 (or 96) years old when his case comes up before the parole board once more. If he lives that long. From the first time he was sentenced for the crime of murder to that date will span seventy-two years. Most of that time has been spent behind bars. More, if the hellish years he spent in a North Dakota reform school are to be counted. And, of course, there is no reason to be sure that he will be released when his case does come back for parole. Although, he says that to be eat a meal at home, and free, is now his greatest wish.

Surely, he regrets his crimes. Surely, he regrets such a wasted life. Indeed, when asked his biggest sadness, Carignan says: 'That I did not learn the meaning of regret earlier in my life.' No regret, we note, for the lives he took and the terrified victims he assaulted. Nevertheless, there is good reason why, when we look at this frail old man, we see want and need nestling in his eyes.

RACHAEL MULLENIX

GAIL BUCKLEY

Teenagers who commit serious crimes aren't as widespread as many people like to think. Certainly, there's the teenage impulse to fight against authority which may result in shoplifting, vandalism or trespassing. This is why, when teenagers commit particularly heinous crimes, the world is shocked by their violence. Males are much more likely to commit crimes of this nature than females - which, once more, makes crimes committed by teenage girls all the more surprising and awful to bear.

Rachael Mullenix rocked the Orange County community, and the entire nation, in 2006 when her crimes came to light. But what was it that drove Rachael to commit the crime that she did? What in her life lead Rachael down such a path of violence, blood, and destruction?

Born in 1989 in Oklahoma City, Rachael was the only child of Barbara and Bruce Mullenix. While she was their own biological child, she did grow up with her half-brother, named Alex. He was a child from Barbara's previous marriage. Rachael grew up in a fairly normal household. She has a stable, normal childhood, perhaps up until the age of 10. It was around then that Rachael's parents began fighting. More importantly, they began fighting in front of her. The marriage was beginning to fall apart right in front of Rachael's eyes.

The happy family fell to alcohol. First, Rachael's father began drinking. This was soon followed by her mother. When Barbara met another person through an extramarital affair, it didn't work out - and the devastation of the failed affair only caused her to drink more. When Rachael was around 13 years old, her parents finally divorced. This was, perhaps, the best thing for the couple. While Bruce Mullenix moved away to Corona for his work, Barbara moved with Rachel to Tampa, Florida.

While Barbara wasn't the perfect mother, there were things in her life that had happened that may have affected her ability to raise her child in the best environment. At the age of eighteen, Barbara was assaulted and became pregnant. She carried her rapist's child to term and put it up for adoption in an effort to give it a good home. Despite a previous marriage and the end of her second, from all that knew her, Barbara was trying her best.

The relationship between Barbara and Rachael was strained. It wasn't exactly a healthy mother-daughter relationship. According to Rachael as she recalled her relationship with her mother, Barbara would become physical with her - scratching her and pulling her hair. There was one time in 2002 when Rachael had the police called on her mother after alleging being bitten by her. The neighbors at the time even observed what they described as a "very apparent" bite mark, in the shape of human teeth. For whatever reason, however, Rachael ended up recanting - whether it was because it never happened, or because Rachael didn't want to invite more ire from her mother, one would never know.

When they lived in Tampa, a sheriff's deputy was dispatched to respond to a 911 call from the townhome that the mother and daughter lived in. The call was in response to an aggravated assault. When he arrived, Barbara was hysterical and crying, and she wouldn't cooperate with the deputy. To him, she seemed incredibly upset and nervous. The deputy also noticed that Barbara was injured, and while she remained, what the deputy called, "uncooperative", he did manage to get out of her that it was Rachael who had attacked her. Despite that, when the deputy called, Rachael simply stated that she and her mother got into an argument and that she left the scene.

According to Rachael, however, Barbara would also make disparaging comments. She would tell her that she would "never amount to anything". After the pair moved to Florida, Barbara quickly ran out of money that would support them. They couldn't stay. When Bruce reached out to reconcile and have Rachael move with him back to California, Rachael agreed - but only if her mother would come with her. Despite their troubles, Rachael was still loyal to her mother. In

2005, the Rachael and Barbara moved back to California and began living with Bruce is his home in Huntington Beach.

Rachael insisted that, despite all of their arguments, she didn't want her mother to be homeless, and that she loved her dearly. So, Bruce and Barbara, now divorced, were once more living together. Where some divorced couples become closer after divorcing, this wasn't the case for Barbara and Bruce Mullenix. They continued fighting, and Barbara continued drinking. It was the drinking that caused Barbara to change into someone else, someone who was not a good mother. Rachael and her mother got along when she was sober, but Rachael tried to stay away from her mother as much as possible when she started drinking.

When Rachael was 17, she met Ian Allen in May of 2006. Ian was, at the time of meeting Rachael, 21. While they began dating, Rachael continued to stay close to her mother. They spent that summer closer than ever, even often getting jobs together as extras on movie sets. Barbara had intentions of living with Rachael after she turned eighteen. Through all of this, Rachael's parents were beginning to accept her boyfriend, Ian. While Rachael was still a minor, their relationship was rocky with the authorities. It prompted Bruce and Barbara to even present Ian with a permission slip to show any authorities that questioned Ian and Rachael's relationship.

Of course, in return for the permission to continue dating their daughter, Rachael was subjected to some rules. She was supposed to be home at by a 1 a.m curfew, as well as other rules of living in their house. As the summer stretched on, Rachael became closer and closer with Ian. As a result, Barbara and Rachael became more and more strained in their relationship. A lot of tension and stress began to swell between mother and daughter. As summer began to draw to a close, Rachael didn't do one of the only things her parents asked of her in regards to dating Ian: she didn't come home on time for her curfew.

On August 31st, 2006, Rachael didn't come home, which threw her mother into a panic. Barbara, like any concerned mother, might do, began to call around frantically looking for her daughter. She called her cell phone, but there was no answer from Rachael. After that, Barbara decided to drive over to Ian's house and see if her daughter was there. She was, and Barbara quite literally dragged Rachael back home. Barbara berated her daughter for breaking her curfew, shouting, "What are you still doing here?" and asking, "Are you on drugs?"

In a diary obtained by the courts, Rachael wrote about the incident. She wrote how she and Ian had awoken at 1:20 in the morning and opened the door to find Barbara standing there. Rachael also wrote about how the incident made her feel "humiliated", and that she wanted to "die right there". According to the diary entry, a week before Barbara had shown up at Ian's place of work and gotten him fired.

After that, Rachael was banned from seeing Ian - though the punishment only lasted a few days. After Rachael begged and pleaded, Barbara finally gave in and allowed Rachael to see a movie with Ian. Ten days later, on September 10th, Rachael once more took to her diary to talk about the way things were going between herself and her mother. She wrote that Barbara is "fucking crazy". Rachael described how Barbara would threaten her daily, as well as Ian. According to Rachael's diary, Barbara was constantly threatening to "do something" to either Rachael or Ian. That same entry went on to talk about how Rachael had "stage one" HPV. Rachael wrote about how Barbara was going to tell Ian's mom about it, and Rachael's anger at Barbara's threat to do that. Rachael's diary entry then mused about how Barbara was going to one day threaten someone she shouldn't, and they would "beat the living shit out of her".

Another entry in the same diary mused about the meaning of life and death, and what it was that kids from "bad homes" did - which, according to Rachael's entry, was "commit murder" and "burn themselves" and "cause harm to others". Rachael's entry then mocks the idea of "turning to God", and she says, "Give me a break." She then says that the only thing that you can do is "try to survive".

On the 8th of September, Ian requested September 12th and 13th off of work, with the explanation that he either needed to help move his girlfriend or his girlfriend's mother - Ian's employer at the time could not explain which when recalling the information. Either way, Ian requested those two specific days off of work. On the 11th of September, Ian made a call to a friend of his by the name of Ryan Wofford, but Wofford only spoke to Ian the following day, on September 12th. Ian discussed with Wofford how he would be leaving work that day and heading to a party and the house of his supervisor. Ian then asked if Wofford would give him a ride home between 2 and 5 a.m. The party was supposed to be in Newport Beach, according to the information that Ian gave Wofford, and that he wanted to drink so he couldn't drive home. After offering to pay for the gas, Wofford reluctantly agreed.

In the early house of the morning on September 13th, between 3 and 3:30 a.m, Ian called Wofford a few times to help direct him to where he wanted to get picked up. It wasn't, as Ian had stated, at a supervisor's house, but rather at the intersection of Corona del Mar. Both Rachael and Ian were waiting for Wofford when he arrived, though it didn't look to him as if either of the two had actually had anything to drink. If they did, it certainly wasn't enough to appear drunk by any stretch of the imagination.

As they drove, Ian helped navigate Wofford to Rachael's house. Despite Wofford driving safely, Ian kept telling him to slow down, not wanting to draw the attention of any police in the area. Despite the warnings, Wofford made it Rachael's house without incident or issue from the police, and the dropped the pair of them off without a problem.

After that, things began to get murky. On September 13th, 2006, a heinous crime occurred and the only people who know exactly what happened are Rachael and Ian.

Earl in the morning, Bruce Mullenix made an attempt to contact Barbara and Rachel the day of September 13th. He was away on a business trip and was trying to call and check in on them. Around the same time, at 9:00 a.m., Ian was making his way to his work site and asked his employer if he could use the dumpster there on site. One of his co-workers observed that Ian seemed "sweaty", like he'd already been up doing work. According to witness co-workers, both Rachael and Ian discarded a number of garbage bags into the dumpsters.

The Newport Beach Police Department found Barbara Mullenix body in the Newport Harbor. As they examined her body, it became clear that she had suffered from more than 50 stab wounds, with three or four different types of knives. In one eye, Barbara still had a butter knife protruding from her body. Her body had been wrapped up in sheets and blankets, and within the bedding, the police retrieved a four-inch pocket knife that had been half closed. Floating near Barbara's body had been a box that had once been used to hold a television. Duct tape had been used to deal the box, and it would later reveal Rachael's DNA on the duct tape.

As investigators made their way to the condo, they found blood on the wall, nightstand, carpet, footboard, and headboard of Barbara's bedroom. The mattress and box spring from the bed was missing, and investigators found Rachael's DNA on the portions of the pillowcases that were not stained with blood. There was more blood to be found on the windowsill next to the stairway, as well as the front door of the condo. Whatever had happened to Barbara here, it was a bloody mess. In the kitchen, there was an open box of latex gloves left on the kitchen counter and green and yellow sponges soaked with blood that had been left out in the bedroom.

Of course, the main suspect in such a crime was Rachael Mullenix - and by association, so was Ian Allen. Ian's ATM card was being monitored by detectives trying to figure out where they were after Barbara's body had been discovered. What they found was that Ian had used his card at a gas station in Sulphur, Louisiana along Interstate 10. But, that was the last place that Ian's card was going to be used because after that he threw both the card and his cell phone away in a trash can at the gas station. It didn't take long for investigators to contact the authorities in Sulphur, and for both Rachael and Ian to be arrested just east of the town.

Rachael told authorities in Louisiana that she had been kidnapped. At the beginning of the interview, Rachael asked them if they knew that she was being kidnapped, and then began to tell the detectives a story about what had happened. According to Rachael, she had fallen asleep sometime between 10 and 11 p.m. on the night of September 12th. When she woke up, it was in the early hours of the morning, and she was startled awake by the sound of Barbara screaming for help. Rachael told the detectives that when she ran into her mother's room, Ian was on top of her and repeatedly stabbing her. Rachael then told the detectives that when she tried to help, Ian threw her off and knocked her out. When she woke up, Barbara was dead and Ian was holding a gun to her head and telling her that she was going to come with him. Rachael claims memory loss and says she only remembers waking up at a place called the Starlight Inn, bound with duct tape.

Rachael denied being part of the murder, despite the eye-witness statements from Ian's co-workers who say them together at Ian's worksite dumping trash bags. When the detectives tried to check with the Starlight Inn, there had been no records that either Ian or Rachael stayed there that night. Still, Rachael claimed that she was being forced at gunpoint to do all of Ian's bidding, saying that he held a gun to her head the entire time she took apart the bed and moved Barbara's body. Rachael also said that she didn't try to run when Ian was checking into motels while she waited in the truck because she was, apparently, afraid for her own life.

Rachael's story might have been believable if eyewitness testimony and DNA evidence wasn't there to paint an entirely different picture.

The investigators who looked over Ian's truck found a .38-caliber revolver that had been wrapped up in a bandana. The gun was stuffed into the driver's side door, and when it was looked over by forensics, it was Rachael's DNA that was found on the gun - while Ian's was there as well, it was mostly Rachael as if she had been the one to handle the gun.

Interviews with the neighbors also found a different story brewing. On the morning of September 13th, between 2:00 and 3:00 in the morning, the neighbor that shared a wall with Barbara Mullenix in their condo had awoken to the sounds of a fight happening on the other side of the wall. He said that there had been a lot of banging, as well as the sound of the sliding glass door being opened. He also told the police that he had heard two female voices and one male voice arguing. Around the same time, a second neighbor had awoken to the commotion and reported hearing the sound of something heavy being dragged outside. When he looked outside, the second neighbor saw Rachael and another person near Barbara's car. Later that morning, around 7:00 a.m, the same neighbor saw Ian return and drive away in his own truck, this time with the trash bags that were discarded at his work site.

When Rachael was returned to California, she pleaded with a Hunting Beach officer was she was being booked for Ian to not be allowed to hurt her. After all of the evidence that was mounting against her, the detectives knew they had to get the right story out of her. Deciding to see if they could get her to slip up, Rachael and Ian were placed together in a patrol car where a recording device had been stashed away and hidden. Left alone for several minutes, the recorder captured Rachael and Ian speaking to one another about the whole ordeal.

Rachael asked Ian if he told the police that he had kidnapped her, and Ian replied that the police didn't believe him when he had told them that. The confessed their love for one another and promised one another that if either of them got out they would come and see the other. It was clear that whatever happened to Barbara Mullenix had been planned by the two of them, and that there was no kidnapping involved. The only crime was one that had been committed by Rachael Mullenix and Ian Allen.

Along with the taped acknowledgment between Rachael and Ian, investigators were also able to recover upwards of 400 or more text messages between both Rachael and Ian between September 10th and 13th. Where Rachael had insisted that she had fallen asleep and woken to the murder already in progress, the text messages told a very different story. Between the Rachael and Ian, text messages spanned most of the night, including between 10:00 pm and 11:00 pm when Rachael said she was sleeping. Rachael gave Ian continuous updates about whether her mother was asleep or not, stating several times that Barbara had either woken up or gone to sleep.

Between 1:45 am and 6:28 a.m, neither Rachael nor Ian exchanged any text messages either with one another or anyone else. It was almost as if there was something that was preoccupying them during those hours. Finally, at 6:28 a.m, Rachael texted Ian to tell him that she loved him, and then again to ask if he was in any trouble - to which Ian simply replied, "Nope".

But why? That was the real question that was burning on everyone's minds as they investigated the case. Sure, Barbara Mullenix was not the best mother at times. She had a drinking problem and would often get into arguments with Rachael about Ian. But what was it that entice Rachael to throw everything away and take her mother's life?

In court, Rachael changed her official testimony about what happened that night with her mother. While the text messages are incriminating, Rachael's changed story about the night of the murder is much different. According to her testimony, Rachael and Ian had a plan of running away. Because Bruce was away on a business trip, Rachael and Ian decided to run away on September 12th, so that they would only have to avoid Barbara. The original plan was to simply wait for Barbara to fall asleep, and then Rachael would leave the condo and meet Ian outside in his truck. However, things didn't go according to plan when Ian entered the condo at 1:45 a.m. Ian and Rachael were talking, and that's what woke Barbara up from her sleep. When Barbara exited her bedroom to find the two of them, Barbara and Ian began arguing. Barbara went to the bedroom to use the phone in there, insisting that she was going to call the police and let them know that Ian was kidnapping her daughter.

That was where the whole night fell apart. Ian followed Barbara into the bedroom, shut the door, and began to attack her. Rachael testified that she attempted to get the fight to stop, and followed the two into Barbara's bedroom to intervene. However, Ian shoved Rachael off and pushed her into a nearby wall. Rachael told the court that after Ian had finished killing Barbara, he shoved her around more and told her to help him clean up, get rid of the body, and hide any of the evidence. Rachael also told the court hat Ian didn't want her to be suspected of helping him kill Barbara, and that's why she originally told the police that she had been kidnapped.

Of course, there are plenty of holes in that story told in court as well. Perhaps the night did begin with a simple plan to run away from home and escalated from there when they were caught. However, the amount of stab wounds and the different kinds of knives that would have made those wounds tells a different story of how Barbara died. There's no way to tell if the crime was one of passion, or if it had been meticulously planned out between Rachael and Ian.

It wasn't until October of 2008 that Rachael Mullenix and Ian Allen were sentenced by a judge. Rachael was 19 by the time she was given her sentence of 25 years to life, and Ian Allen 23 when he was convicted of first-degree murder. Bruce Mullenix stood by Rachael's side during the entire trial, and even the years afterward. He insisted that it was Barbara who was a raging alcoholic and that his daughter could never have done something so heinous. At her sentencing, Rachael, too, continued to stick to her story: that she had been planning to run away the night that her mother was killed, and that something tipped Ian over too far into murdering her. Rachael said that every day without her mother was "a struggle", and that she would "never take responsibility for it". She told the judge at her sentencing that if she had done it, "[her] family would be the first to know".

During his own trial, Ian Allen changed his own story, as well. He insisted that it was Rachael who had done the deed of murdering Barbara and that he was just an observer of the aftermath. Had Rachael originally convinced him to take the fall for her, or had it been Ian all along? There was no way to tell what had really happened, except that Barbara had been brutally murdered and only Rachael and Ian knew the truth of why and how. At her sentencing, the Judge did not feel that Rachael showed the appropriate remorse for her actions, despite Rachael insisting that she had been taught as a young child to hide her emotions because of her mother's verbal abuse.

Still, Rachael insisted that she loved her mother and that there was no way that she could kill her. At their separate trials, Rachael and Ian pointed the blame at one another. There was only the evidence that they had both been in the room and that they had both tried to clean up the aftermath of what had happened. Who stabbed the knives into Barbara's body could not be determined but by their own statements. Whether or not Rachael was the one who plunged the knife into her mother's body, or whether or not she had convinced Ian to do it, it was Rachael who brought Ian into her mother's life and, in the end, stood by Ian's side when her mother's life ended. A jury of her peers convicted Rachael of first-degree murder and a judge sentenced her to 25 to life for the crime that Rachael Mullenix, still, insists she did not commit.

ALYSSA BUSTAMANTE
MAGGIE RAWLS

Alyssa Bustamante came from a troubled family. It sparked a rage inside of her that led to one of the most shocking killings in recent memory.

Born to Michelle and Ceaser Bustamante on January 28th, 1994, her parents were cousins by marriage and her mother was only fifteen years old. They moved around the state of California before moving all the way to St. Martins, Missouri when Alyssa was two years old. Michelle wanted to be near her mother, Karen Brooke, who lived in nearby Jefferson City.

Michelle would give birth to a set of twin boys four years after Alyssa and then have another daughter. The teen mother couldn't adequately provide for her young children, however, compiling a record of petty thefts to support a drug habit. Michelle struggled to pay the rent and found herself with three misdemeanor criminal convictions for drunk driving and marijuana possession. Ceaser was even worse, routinely beating Michelle before receiving a ten-year prison sentence for an undisclosed assault charge.

"She (Alyssa) had a very troubled background," Jefferson City reporter Jeff Haldiman said. "A very troubled life. Her mother and father both had issues with drugs and drinking."

At the age of six years old, a hungry Alyssa would walk into her living room and see her mother stretched out on the couch.

Drunk and high.

"Alyssa's mother was not much to write home about," forensic psychologist Paula Orange said. "She would do drugs in from of Alyssa, one time to the point of overdosing in front of her. She would also leave the little girl to fend for herself a lot. She was the type that would say 'there's cereal and milk in the fridge.'"

The sight of her mother down and out on drugs, the absent father, and the daily neglect would prove to be too traumatic for Alyssa.

"Something in her snapped, early on her childhood," Orange said. "There are numerous stories where children are able to overcome horrendous parenting. Alyssa received a lot of help but couldn't do it."

Child protective services would eventually intervene on Alyssa's behalf. They would remove her from her mother's custody and sent to live with her grandmother.

Her grandmother, Karen Brooke, was excited to give Alyssa a second chance at life.

"The grandmother was put in charge taking care of Alyssa and her brothers and her sister by court order due to issues that Alyssa's mother had over the years," Cole County Sheriff Greg White said.

It took some time but Karen would eventually be given legal guardianship over Alyssa and her other siblings in 2002. The children would enjoy living at their grandparents' house which was on a large ranch. There was plenty of room for the children to play both on the ranch lot and in the woods nearby.

The intervention on Alyssa's behalf, however, had come too late.

LIKE MOTHER, LIKE DAUGHTER

As she got older, Alyssa would replicate the life of her mother.

She would pop pills...Tylenol, Thorazine, whatever else she could get her hands on...then lose herself in violent fantasies and suicidal thoughts.

By the age of thirteen, those suicidal ideations would come full bore as she overdosed on some psych meds mixed with some over the counter drugs.

"It was a Labor Day weekend," Haldiman said. "When she had taken an overdose and was found in the bathroom. I think that was one of the bigger warning signs for the grandmother to try and get more help for her."

"She took a bunch of Tylenol and something else," Alyssa's friend, Jennifer Meyer said. "Some sort of pain killer. This was at her grandparent's home. She passed out and her grandma found her and called an ambulance. She had to have her stomach pumped. Then she went to the hospital for awhile and they sent her to a psych ward for awhile. I know she was away from school for like two or three months."

The suicide attempt was an alarming wake-up call for Karen Brook. Alyssa was only thirteen. Teenagers trying to commit suicide certainly wasn't uncommon among teens with troubled backgrounds, but even physicians commented that they never encountered someone as young as Alyssa with her kind of thoughts.

Karen would seek help from as many third parties as she could. She would send Alyssa to several different therapists as well as a psychiatrist who started her on anti-depressants.

A DOUBLE LIFE

Despite her inner turmoil, Alyssa was a stellar student. She never took a day off from school and got nothing less than "B" grades in school. Her teachers recognized her intelligence and she did not appear to have any discipline problems.

"If you had a face to face conversation with her," White said. "You would say to yourself that this is a good choice for a babysitter. She came across very well."

Alyssa, however, had a double life.

She would play the part of the nice high school girl during the day with conservative fashion and make-up. This fooled the teachers and counselors.

But outside of school, this would change.

Alyssa could contort her face into a hard look. She had pale blue eyes which she accented with heavy black eyeliner, drawn into a Kabuki-style triangle, giving her a clownish look. She had light brown hair which sometimes ran down into her eyes. She had plenty of attitude and ran with a Goth crowd.

She fostered this alter-ego on-line, cyber-bullying people for recreation. On her social media sites, she would smear red lipstick which she made to look like vampire blood. She would snarl at the camera and grit her teeth.

SELF-MUTILATION

The angry and bizarre poses on her social media masked a bigger problem. Alyssa hated herself and wanted to cause self-harm. She would take razor blades and make incisions on her arm and wrist.

Psychologists would see this act as a form of self-medication.

Alyssa would carve pentagrams, hearts with a line going through them, and an upside down "Peace" sign. Her largest work was carving the word "HATE" across her belly in large letters.

She would do this cutting as a form of distraction. She would focus on the blade cutting into her skin, the blood coming out...and the pain. She did this as a way to take the focus off her emotional difficulties and make physical pain take center stage.

"The cutting would give her a temporary respite," Orange said. "Alyssa would find herself coming off the high of cutting herself and eventually the bad memories, bad situations, would arise once again in her mind, forcing her to cut herself again. It would become an endless cycle of self-harm."

By the time she was a teenager, Alyssa would amass over three-hundred self-inflicted cuts all over her body. She would also burn herself with matches and bite into her skin.

"There was another side to her," White said. "It was like flipping a switch, going back and forth between the two."

"It was almost like she was living two different lives," Haldiman said. "But inside something was building up. Really building up."

AN ON-LINE PRESENCE OF RED FLAGS

Alyssa would showcase her person on-line as 'badalyssa' among other pseudonyms. In one social media profile, she listed her hobbies as "cutting" and "killing people". These were more than words of bravo from an attention seeking teenager.

Alyssa meant every word.

Her YouTube account was registered under the name Okamikage which was Japanese for "Wolfshadow." She listed her location as "somewhere I don't want to be" and her profile photo showed her with the vampire-style lipstick, pointing a finger at her head like a gun.

Scars from her cutting could be seen on her wrist.

Her YouTube channel (since removed) featured several videos of both her and her brothers trying to replicate stunts they had seen in the show "Jackass". The one revealing video, however, is one that Alyssa titled "Idiots Getting Electrocuted by Electric Fence."

The video starts with Alyssa filming herself touching an electrified fence used to house cattle. She laughs and shudders at the jolt then begins coercing her younger brothers to follow her lead.

"This is where it gets good," Alyssa wrote on the YouTube video clip. "This is where my brothers get hurt."

Her Twitter messages were all dark and more than hinted at an inner rage. She wrote often of "addiction" and "terrors."

"All I want in life is a reason for all his pain," she tweeted as well as "I hate authority."

While in school, she would freak out her friends by asking bizarre questions.

"You ever wonder what it would be like to kill someone?"

But most of her friends would not take her seriously. It seemed as it seemed like idle teenage banter.

"I was at her party," Alyssa's friend Jennifer Meyer said. "And she kind of just took me off to the side randomly and she's like, 'You know, I wonder what it would be like to kill somebody,' because I guess she was mad at one of her friends there, but it just seemed kind of strange. But you wouldn't logically think one of your friends would kill somebody."

Alyssa seemed to be building herself up psychologically to kill someone, The questions and conversations with friends allowing her to psyche herself up for something she wanted to do.

"I'd like to kill her," Alyssa would say, pointing at a random person walking down the hallway at school.

Her words would eventually lead to the deed.

THE MOST INNOCENT

Just leaving a few houses down, nine-year-old Elizabeth Olten would come over to Alyssa's house to play with Alyssa's half-sister.

Elizabeth was a sweet-faced girl with a personality to match. She loved cats, the color pink and was a "girly girl." She had long brown hair and sparkling brown eyes. She was shy but friendly.

"She was somebody special," Peggy Florence said, a friend of the family. "They call her a girlie girl. She would be outside in the snow or in the mud in her frilly little dress."

"Everything that I could tell about Elizabeth," White said. "Was that she was a sweet young lady who did relatively well at school. Her classmates seemed to like her. The teachers had good reports and her mom and family loved her dearly."

"She had frequently gone to the five-year old's (Alyssa's sister) residence," White said. "So it wasn't a huge issue."

Everyone loved Elizabeth.

Everyone except Alyssa as she watched the two girl play act with dolls on the back porch, having a "tea party."

Alyssa eyeballed the young Elizabeth with one thing on her mind. She wanted to kill her.

"I think Alyssa chose Elizabeth predominantly because it was a relatively easy target of opportunity," White said. "And that's a horrid thing."

THE KILLING TIME

In the fall of 2009, Alyssa began planning out how and when she would fulfill her sick fantasy.

She walked into the woods behind her house and began digging.

Plugging in her ear buds while listening to some death metal, she dug and dug, digging two shallow graves.

"She'd been thinking of killing for some time," White said. "And certainly had started to take significant steps toward accomplishing that end."

Alyssa dug the graves out three feet deep. Police would later speculate that she initially wanted to kill her two younger brothers and that the two shallow graves were for them. They pointed to the YouTube video in which she displayed sadistic delight in torturing her brothers by the electric fence. But when an opportunity presented itself in the form of Elizabeth Olten, she took advantage.

"Alyssa didn't care about anyone," Orange said. "Anyone or anything. She was depressed and anti-social. She hated society. She hated people."

Alyssa's diary would confirm her hatred of people and anti-social mindset. On the days leading to the murder, she would write about her cell phone battery dying. There was one long entry where Alyssa would complain about that fact that she could not call anyone to talk about the depression and rage she felt.

"If I don't talk about it," Alyssa wrote. "I bottle it up and when I explode, someone's going to die."

During this time, Karen Brooke would become increasingly worried about Alyssa. A religious woman, Karen realized that all of the counseling, therapy and medication was having no effect on Alyssa. Her granddaughter was still cutting herself and her physician raised her dose of Prozac to forty milligrams a day.

Karen would complain that the high dosage would have an altering effect on Alyssa's behavior. She would come home late when she normally would come straight home after school. She would not come down for the family evening meals, leaving her grandmother to worry about her mental state. Karen would then call Alyssa's doctor and he informed her that the higher dosage of the Prozac would take another month "to level out."

But the Prozac would have no effect on Alyssa. On October 21st, 2009, she would bring her morbid fantasies to life.

AFRAID OF THE DARK

It was starting to get dark. Elizabeth knew she had to get home or else her mother would get mad.

She said her goodbyes to her playmate then started to walk home.

Then she received a call on her cell phone.

It was Alyssa.

"Come back to the house," Alyssa said. "I have a surprise for you."

The girl trekked back to the home and Alyssa led her down the wooded path behind her home. The two walked for quite a ways before Elizabeth started to become tired and scared.

"It's getting dark," Elizabeth complained. "I want to go home."

"Don't you want your surprise?" Alyssa asked.

Elizabeth trusted Alyssa. She was older and seemed nice.

"I don't know."

"Come on, you're going to love it."

"Okay."

Alyssa put her arm around Elizabeth and led her further into the woods. The two walked and walked until the sky grew dark.

Without warning, Alyssa began to attack Elizabeth.

"Alyssa began by trying to cut Elizabeth's throat," White said. "And Elizabeth reached up and grabbed the knife, receiving defensive wounds on the inside of her fingers. Alyssa ends up dropping the knife and begins trying to strangle Elizabeth. According to her statement to us, strangling her until 'the light went out in her eyes.' And then she's down, kneeling across Elizabeth's torso and takes the knife and stabs her eight times. One time sufficiently hard to go through the breastbone, through the top part of the heart into her spine."

"This was her kill fantasy," Orange said. "That is why she tried all three methods of killing. First, she tried slicing Elizabeth's throat. Perhaps that didn't give her the feeling she craved so she began strangling the girl to death. But she needed more. She needed to know what all those fantasies felt like. So then she began stabbing the young girl. Slicing, strangling, and stabbing. She had thought about all three and wanted to know what they all felt like."

The self-harm, the self-mutilation that she practiced on herself was now transferred to harming someone else.

Someone innocent.

Her adrenaline racing, Alyssa dragged Elizabeth's body to one of the shallow graves.

"Alyssa took Elizabeth's body and rolled it to the grave and covered it up," White said. "Stringed some leaves across it and went home. Got cleaned up. Put the knife in the dishwasher."

A HAPPY KILLER

The next morning, Alyssa would write out her thoughts in her journal, expressing the euphoria at what she had done. She described how she had just killed someone, strangled them and slit their throat.

"It was ahmazing," Alyssa would write, going on to say how much she enjoyed it then ending the entry with a snarky "Kay,I gotta go to church now, lol."

Elizabeth's mother had called the police around seven p.m., about forty-five minutes after she was last seen. The community organized quickly.

The search began quickly for the girl. St. Martins, Missouri epitomized small town America. It had just over one thousand people and everyone knew each other. Volunteers began searching the woods behind the neighborhood homes.

Police pinged Elizabeth's cell phone and the GSP led them to the woods but the battery on Elizabeth's cell gave out.

The authorities knew they were close but they could not find Elizabeth.

Alyssa had done a very good job of hiding the body.

"Elizabeth was already dead before we were ever notified," White said. "It was that fast."

Everyone in town thought that an older male predator had snatched up Elizabeth.

"That was the narrative that everyone was used to," Orange said. "Everyone became frantic, talking about any strangers that they may have seen in town. But soon rumors spread that a teenager was involved. Everyone assumed it to be a teenage male."

RETRACING ELIZABETH'S STEPS

Alyssa had not shown up for school the day after Elizabeth's abduction. It was her first unexcused absence.

This raised a red flag to police as they questioned Alyssa. They brought her out back where they asked why she had dug out a grave.

Then they began searching through the house.

Alyssa acted fast. She tried to block what she had written in the diary by scratching out the words.

"We were still able to read some of the words through the writing," White said. "We put a very strong light source behind it and read her original words. At that point, she did confess to it and ultimately take us to the scene of the homicide and to the grave."

Word spread around town that Elizabeth was dead and that Alyssa was the killer.

Everyone involved went into shock. A senseless crime, a murder of an innocent.

Did this really happen?

The brutality of the crime shocked the community. An adult killing a child is rare but it has happened before. No one had ever heard of a fifteen-year-old girl killing a nine-year-old.

"When they announced they had found the body," Haldiman said. "There was an audible hush. They just couldn't believe that, nobody could believe that, number one a child was dead and number two that the person that did it was as young as she was. That just floored so many people. Everybody."

The case became even more tragic as only weeks earlier a panel of psychiatrists determined that Alyssa should be institutionalized for a long term. These clinicians knew that Alyssa was an extreme danger to both herself and other people.

Their warnings went unheeded, however, and Alyssa was returned home.

THE TRIAL

Alyssa would be put to trial and be tried as an adult.

"In this case," White said. "It was clearly, coldly planned, calculated and executed. She executed her neighbor for no reason other than she wanted to see someone die."

While awaiting trial, Alyssa went stir crazy behind bars. She began cutting herself with her own fingernails before placed on suicide watch. Her attorney motioned that she be sent to a psychiatric institution.

Her defense team worked overtime to try and explain Alyssa's murderous act. They recounted the fact that she had been on the anti-depressant Prozac and had been told to increase her dosage a few weeks before murdering the little girl. They told the jury about her upbringing of neglect, suicide attempts and the mental illnesses/drug use of both parents.

But the community-at-large wanted Alyssa's blood. Among the things they wrote were:

"What is a shame is that the Murderer did not die when she tried to commit suicide when she tried to in 2007."

"From what I've heard this girl has had mental problems for some time and has seen counselors or someone in the past."

"Either deport her or send her to the gas chamber. One less sicko wasting our tax dollars."

Prosecutor Mark Richardson would argue for Alyssa to receive life in prison plus an additional seventy-one years.

The years that Elizabeth had lost.

"These sentences are appropriate," Richardson wrote. "And fit what happened to Elizabeth at the hands of a truly evil individual who strangled and stabbed an innocent child simply for the thrill of it."

Alyssa would plead guilty to second-degree murder.

She would take the stand during her trial and betray some signs of humanity, turning to Elizabeth's mother and family.

She expressed how "horribly" she felt for what she had done. Then she suggested that if she could give her own life for Elizabeth's, she would.

The apology fell on deaf ears for both Elizabeth's family and the jury. They felt as if the apology was fake and meaningless.

"I think Alyssa should get out of jail the same day Elizabeth gets out of the grave!", screamed Elizabeth Olten's grandmother.

"She's an evil monster," Elizabeth's mother, Patty Preiss said. "So much has been lost at the hands of this evil monster. Elizabeth was given a death sentence, and we were given a life sentence. I hate her. I hate everything about her. She's not even human."

"Alyssa was pure evil," Orange said. "She told investigators that she killed Elizabeth, that darling little girl, because she wanted to see the light in her eyes go out. If that doesn't make her evil and irredeemable, I don't know what does."

"When a person plans and executes for no other reason that they want to see another person die," White said. "That person is going to re-offend. I think Alyssa is too dangerous to be out of prison."

Alyssa would be sentenced to life in prison but given the possibility of parole. She currently resides in a Missouri women's prison.

Elizabeth would receive the funeral of a beloved princess. Her casket was placed inside a horse-drawn carriage.

All of her friends and family wore her favorite color: pink.

WHEN THE GIRL NEXT DOOR KILLS: THE TRUE STORY OF TYLAR WITT

ERICA FOSTER

"At round one in the morning, the girl snuck the boy into her house. He stabbed her in her sleep, killing her and freeing themselves." This was an excerpt from fourteen year old Tylar Witt's story entitled, "The Killer and his Raven." A story she wrote about her own mother's brutal murder.

Tylar Witt lived in an upscale neighborhood in El Dorado Hills, California with her forty seven year old single mother, Joanne Witt. Joanne worked for the county as an assistant engineer for the Department of Transportation and they lived in an elegant house in a nice gated community. Tylar was a fourteen year old girl who was entering her freshman year at Oak Ridge High School. She was described as a sweet girl when she was growing up. Her mother paid for riding lessons and they liked to stay at home and watch movies and cook, but as Tylar grew up, the behavioral problems began and the fights between the mother and daughter turned into physical altercations. Tylar was turning into a different person, she was becoming a monster.

It all started out as what looked like typical teenage rebellion. Tylar embraced the emo and gothic lifestyle by wearing dark and baggy clothes, she had a love of anime and Japanese cartoons, along with everything violent and connected with death. Tylar met her 'Romeo', nineteen year old Steven Colver, at a coffee shop in the popular shopping center of Town Center Shops, where they both frequented. As Tylar was entering her first year of high school, Steven was beginning his first year of college. He was employed as a Shift Lead at Rubio's Mexican Grill. The duo quickly became inseparable. Tylar looked at the older boy as a god and worshiped everything about him. There wasn't anything she wouldn't do for him. The two were in love.

It was in April of 2009, a few weeks after the two had met, that Tylar approached her mother. She convinced her mother that Steven was gay, so that he would be allowed to rent the extra room in their family home. After much resistance from family and friends, Joanne defended the decision by saying that Steven would be helping her make the mortgage payment, as well as help Tylar with her homework. She was described as very strong-willed by her friends and family and didn't let their opinion of others affect her decision to let Steven move in. Joanne didn't suspect a relationship between Steven and her daughter until one day in May, about a month after Steven had moved in. She entered Steven's room and found Steven and Tylar about to engage in a sexual relationship, or had just finished. She found Tylar naked and hiding in Steven's closet, trying to cover herself up. Joanne was understandably upset and demanded that Steven immediately move out. She called two of her male coworkers to come over and assist her. Joanne informed them that she was kicking Steven out of her house and she didn't want to be alone when she did it in case anything were to happen. The male coworkers helped place all of Steven's belongings on the sidewalk and even threatened Steven before he left.

Vinnie Capatano, one of Joanne's coworkers helping her that day, threatened Steven, "If you make contact with Tylar again, either by phone or in person- I am going to hurt you. And I am going to hurt you East Coast style, not West Coast style." It was an act intended to promote intimidation and scare tactics. Steven looked unshaken, which annoyed Capatano even further. His words didn't seem to bother Steven at all.

Joanne was convinced that Steven had committed a crime by sleeping with her underage daughter and made that clear to Steven before he left. She threatened to go to the police and file statutory rape charges if Steven ever came into contact with her daughter again. He didn't take Joanne's words seriously, or the threats of her coworkers. Steven was later found at least twenty more times after this encounter, sneaking into Joanne's house. All Joanne wanted to do was get her daughter away from this older boy that seemed to influence her bad behavior and irrational decisions. Joanne acted as any other mother in this situation would.

Despite the threats, Steven and Tylar continued their love affair and sexual relationship during the day while Joanne was at work and late at night while Joanne was sleeping. Joanne had expressed concern to a few of her coworkers about her daughter's behavior and the boy that seemed able to control and influence her so greatly. It wasn't long until Joanne found out what was going on behind her back and continued to make good on her promise of going to the police. Steven and Tylar vowed to find a way to stay together, no matter the cost. This is the moment the plotting began between the modern day Romeo and Juliet. This was about a month before Joanne Witt was found dead in her home and arrest warrants were issued for her daughter and her daughter's boyfriend.

Joanne Witt located her daughter's diary and handed it over to the police that were handling the statutory rape complaint. The diary clearly outlined the sexual relationship between Tylar Witt and Steven Colver. It explicitly described numerous sexual positions and encounters that the two had shared. There was no mistaking that there was definitely a sexual relationship happening between Steven and Tylar. The detective called to interview Steven about the allegations and Steven claimed that he was worried about Tylar, but their relationship was platonic. He said he considered Tylar as more of a sister figure, than anything else, and he denied any sexual relationship between the two of them. He also admitted that he was scared of this whole situation and he knew she was only fourteen years old. The relationship between Tylar and her mother was volatile and destructive, to say the least, even before she turned in the diary.

Joanne was a loving and attentive single mother that made her daughter, Tylar, the center of her world. However, an incident that took place when Tylar was five years old, prompted an investigation that removed her only daughter from her home. Tylar was placed into foster care for a brief time before Joanne's parents, Norb and Judi Witt could take her in. Tylar lived with them for 6 months while Joanne attended anger management and parenting classes. The incident occurred when Tylar was just five years old after

Joanne had picked her up from daycare. The young girl was screaming in the backseat which was causing Joanne to lose patience very quickly. Joanne reached back and slapped Tylar. The daycare saw the hand shaped mark on Tylar and immediately reported the abuse to CPS, Child Protective Services.

After Tylar was finally able to go back home to her mother, Joanne was afraid to discipline her like she had before. This gave Tylar the opportunity to do whatever she wanted, knowing she could get away with it. Tylar would threaten to call CPS and report her mother again if she didn't get what she wanted. This created many behavioral problems for Tylar and this manifested itself in the violent relationship between the mother and the daughter. Tylar also reported that her mother was a heavy drinker and she would hit and punch Tylar when she was mad. These allegations were never proven. If the violence and abuse had been as severe as Tylar had made it sound, there would have been noticeable marks and bruises on Tylar. They never found any evidence of the abuse she claimed was taking place at the home. There was constant fighting and arguing. Joanne didn't feel comfortable enough start disciplining her daughter again until the few months before that led up to her murder.

The day that Joanne admitted to taking her daughter's diary into the police, was the same night that Joanne and Tylar got into a horrendous fight at home. Tylar felt betrayed by her mother's actions and began throwing objects at her and fighting with her. Tylar called 911 pretending to be Joanne in an attempt to be taken out of the home. She would have rather been in the Juvenile Detention Center than at home with her mother that night. Joanne got onto the phone with dispatch and when they asked her if she was okay, she responded no. Deputies were on their way to the residence. When the police arrived they saw a cut on Joanne's chin and several bruises. Tylar was taken in that night but was released only hours later, after Joanne refused to press charges against her daughter. Joanne was never required to go to the hospital due to her injuries.

Norbert Witt, Tylar's grandfather, claimed that Steven was a bad influence on his granddaughter, and said that he corrupted her by exposing her to sex and heavy narcotics. Steven was known to engage in illegal narcotics such as marijuana, ecstasy, and cocaine.

Norb and Judi Witt owned a luxury RV and had spent the previous two months traveling around the country. They arrived home only days before they received the call that would turn their world upside down. It was Monday when they received a call from Joanne's boss inquiring if they had any idea as to the whereabouts of their daughter. Joanne had an impeccable work history and never missed work without first calling to let them know. So, when Joanne didn't show up or call that Friday, her coworkers began to worry. They stopped by her home that night and knocked on the door, but there was no answer. Nobody seemed to be home. After Joanne didn't show up to work the following Monday either, they knew something was terribly wrong and called the police to report Joanne as missing. After speaking to Joanne's parents and informing them that they had already contacted the police, they raced over to their daughter's house, which was only a few miles away, so they could check themselves. It is there that they met the police. Norb Witt let them into the house to search. The police informed Joanne's parents that she was found upstairs in her room, and she was deceased. There was no sign of a break in or forced entry, there was nothing missing in the home. But where was Tylar? Better yet, where were Tylar and her older boyfriend?

It didn't take the police long to realize that Tylar and Steven had something to do with the cruel and heinous crime in the Witt house. It was only weeks earlier that Joanne had reported Steven to the police and turned in Tylar's diary. She made her feelings about her mother known in the words scrawled throughout the pages. Tylar even plastered her contempt for her mother across her social media sites. She wasn't shy when it came to sharing her feelings and opinion of her mother.

Tylar and Steven went on like normal the days following the murder. They were living the life they wanted now that Tylar's mother wasn't there to get in the middle of it and stop it. They were seen holding hands and kissing, and had seen some of their friends. It was after a night of smoking marijuana and doing lines of cocaine at Steven's father's house that Steven confessed to murdering Joanne and even showed his friend the bloody knife that he was hiding in the car. This friend was Matthew Wildman. Wildman later testified against Steven and told the court that Steven did indeed show him the knife that was used, and he described how the murder happened, and how Steven stood there when he was finished and watched Joanne die. Steven's father came home unexpectedly so they all left the house, with the murder weapon. The murder weapon was never retrieved after their arrest.

The couple had fled to San Francisco, they no longer cared about the consequences because their plan all along was to commit suicide. If they weren't there, they wouldn't have to face the murder charges. According to their logic, that was the only way that they would be able to stay together, without interference, as well as keep Steven out of jail because of the statutory rape charges. They thought the charges would carry a heavy prison sentence and they didn't want to risk separation due to the diary that Joanne had turned into the police earlier.

While in San Francisco, they rented a hotel room and consumed a bazaar mix of fruit loops, cake and rat poison and each had written out suicide notes. The combination of food mixed with the rat poison didn't work, however, and they were arrested shortly after, before they had a second chance to commit suicide. Alongside the food that was found in the hotel room, police also found marijuana, condoms, Steven's work apron and nametag, and the movie 'Donnie Darko' on DVD. They were found changing clothes behind a dumpster at a shopping mall in the area and were arrested by local police and taken in for questioning regarding Joanne Witt's murder.

Once in custody, Tylar refused to admit that she knew her mother was dead and admitted no fault. She asked for a lawyer and for the detectives to go away. The fateful night her mother was brutally murdered was June 11, 2009. Well into the night, after Joanne had finally fallen asleep, Tylar let Steven into the house. He had acquired a chef's knife from his restaurant job at Rubio's. Tylar had grabbed a knife out of the kitchen in her house, and the two proceeded to go upstairs to the bedroom where Joanne Witt was fast asleep. They had each planned to use the knives they had to kill Joanne....together. Tylar claimed that she could not go into the room with Steven. She fell to her knees and covered her ears, while humming to drown out the sound of her mother being stabbed to death. Steven had taken several practice slashes in the air as a warm up before going into Joanne's room and Tylar said this is what prompted her to stay outside of the room. She chose not to go in with Steven. Joanne was stabbed around twenty times. The fatal wound was a gaping slash in her neck. She struggled with her killer and had put her hands up in defense but the wounds were too severe. A bloody knife outline was left on the bed and a book entitled, "How to Parent your Out-Of-Control Teenager, was ironically nestled in the nightstand next to her bed. Tylar and Steven covered Joanne's body with a blanket, turned the air conditioner down in an attempt to preserve the body, and locked up the house and left. They decided to jump the fence instead of having to put the code in to get out. They didn't want anyone to place them there at the time of the murder.

In a suicide letter that Steven had written to his friends, as a kind of apology for what he had done, he said, "Our souls are tainted...We shall be awaiting our fate in the afterworld."

After the news of Joanne's murder got around, a neighbor spoke up about allegedly speaking to Tylar in the park a few months prior. The neighbor had been walking her daughter to the park and claimed she saw a young girl that looked alone, sad, and even angry. The girl was sitting on the swing set with her face toward the ground. She confronted her and asked what was wrong. She said the girl described a bad home life with her mother, and mentioned that her mother liked to drink and would get violent and hurt her, and they would get into a lot of fights. She said the girl seemed really cold and lost in her replies. When asked what Tylar was going to do to stop it the next time it happened she simply replied, "There isn't going to be a next time. Next time it is going to be either her or me." This statement stuck with the neighbor for a long time after. When she realized that the crime scene was a daughter that killed her mother, she finally spoke to police about the conversation in the park. The neighbor was seen on news footage talking to one of the police on the scene, but requested that her name be left out of the media.

Dan Weiner, Steven's attorney, claimed that it was not Steven that committed the murder, it was Tylar. When describing her relationship with Steven, Tylar said, "I trusted him more than I trusted anyone. And I love him more than anybody or anything. If he told me to jump off a bridge and I asked him why and he said just trust me, I would have done it." This shows just how much influence Steven had over Tylar. When neighbors of Steven's were asked to describe him they had only nice things to say.

"He's always been a nice kid as far as I am concerned. If this is true, it is out of character." –Paul Matloff. He also described Steven as a stand-up kid that never played his music too loudly and was always eager to help his neighbors.

Joan Colver, Steven's mother was quoted by reporters as saying, "He would care about others before himself. Steven is the kind of guy who would drive off a cliff or jump in front of a bullet or run into a burning building....for a friend."

When asked why Weiner felt that Steven was being targeted for performing the actual murder instead of Tylar, he didn't really know why. He backed up his defense and Steven's statement of Tylar being the one to murder Joanne Witt, given her past history compared to Steven's.

"He has never hurt anybody, or tried to hurt anybody or threatened to hurt anybody. As contrasted with Tylar who has a very specific history with her mother, and has literally threatened to kill her, to stab her...the very method by which she was ultimately killed!"

Steven had changed his story and said that Joanne was already dead by the time he arrived at the Witt house that night.

"I think realizing the gravity of the situation after being in jail for a while, it took a while before he was willing to confirm, yeah, that she had done it and how she had done it." Steven said that Tylar stabbed her own mother to death and then called him over to the house after it was done. That is when he claims to have seen the bloody knife. He said that there was blood dripping everywhere, including some spots on Tylar's pants, but there was no evidence of blood droplets being found anywhere else in the house. It was all confined to Joanne's bedroom where she was murdered. The defense claimed that the police failed to look for blood anywhere else except for the primary focus of the house, which was the bedroom. Therefore, there was no evidence available to back up Steven's story. This new story also came about after Steven had already described to his friends how he stabbed his girlfriend's mother to death in her sleep with a butcher knife. Weiner said that Steven was not homicidal, rather suicidal. They claimed that the plan was for Steven to pick up Tylar and they would run off to San Francisco for a few days and then commit suicide together. There was no talk of murdering Joanne. The defense also mentioned that Steven had a clean record, while Tylar's was filled with a history of violence and running away. Despite the new story, Steven's confession to his friend was more than the prosecution needed. He was convicted based on his own words, just as his mother had predicted earlier.

In prosecutor Lisette Suder's words in her opening statement at trial, she described the couple's actions as "a

19 year old man and a 14 year old girl and their love affair that led to the violent almost to the point of sadistic murder of her mother." Tylar was portrayed as an extremely manipulative and brilliant girl. After lying to the detectives when she was first taken into custody and questioned, she finally decided to tell the truth and later passed a polygraph test proving it. She admitted to conspiring with Steven to kill her mother, but also said that it was Steven that committed the actual murder, while she lay in a fetal position outside of the bedroom. All of the evidence found on the scene corroborated Tylar's account of the events from that night. Tylar, in exchange for her testimony against Steven, received a reduced sentence of fifteen years to life for second degree murder. She would be eligible for parole at the age of twenty nine, instead of thirty nine. They were both sentenced at the El Dorado County Superior Court in Placerville.

Joanne Witt's brother, Michael, shared his feelings before sentencing. He was the one that had been responsible for cleaning up his sister's home after the murder. He said he would never be able to get the images of the crime scene photos out of his head.

"I hope and desire that Mr. Colver experiences the worst possible experiences our wonderful prison system can bestow upon him." The judge had tried several times to stop Matthew's rant.

The trial began with Steven still trying to protect Tylar. He didn't want people to accuse his love, Tylar, of being the mother killer. In the beginning stages of his questioning he would ask investigators if they had spoken with Tylar and he inquired about her well-being. He was sympathetic to her situation and just wanted to help her. He thought they were in it together and their love would keep them connected. It ended with the scorned lovers passing the blame to each other. Steven's defense referred to him as an easily manipulated love-struck teen.

Steven's trial lasted for four weeks but the verdict only took four hours to come back. With Tylar's account of the events, the confession Steven made to his friends, and the DNA found underneath Joanne's fingernails that linked the homicide to a male attacker, it all led Steven to a verdict of guilty, for first degree murder. He was sentenced to life in prison without the possibility of parole.

After sentencing, however, Tylar had an interview in which she admitted, "I still have a really hard time being honest. I panic when I get in trouble and the first thing I want to do is lie to get out of it." This statement could potentially be enough to seek an appeal for Steven Colver at a later date. It showed just how dishonest Tylar could be. So if she were able to say this now, what if everything she said in the trial was a lie, despite the polygraph test.

Tylar's psychologist referred to her as a sociopath. Tylar, in trial, said she had three different personalities that were living inside of her. She had her own personality, an angel named Alex, and a demon she referred to as Toby. She claimed her violent actions that led up to this point were because of the demon. Toby would come in times of intense stress. Tylar also described blackouts that she would experience when she was enraged and tried to use the compassion of her dead mother to sway the jury in her favor.

"My mom was not a vicious person and she didn't hold grudges. Even if something horrible like this would have happened, she would have asked for a just punishment. She wouldn't want to see someone suffer for the rest of their lives for a mistake they made when they were being ignorant and stupid."

The following is a letter that Tylar allegedly wrote to her mother before she was murdered. It was Tylar's plan to run away and commit suicide. It was a good bye letter addressed to Joanne.

"As much as you don't think I love you, I do. Not just because I am your daughter but because you are my best friend. Nothing I have ever said to you in anger was ever true. I would never kill you or hate you....but I can't stand to see you so unhappy, but I am growing up and seeing as you don't love me....the person I have become, I see it only fit I do one last thing to make you happy. You want me gone? I am gone."

In Tylar's testimony she admitted the act of violence toward her mother was not a spontaneous decision. It was a decision Steven and Tylar had made after thoroughly discussing their options.

"I was in shock and then I went into a full blown panic attack, hyperventilating, screaming, and shaking." This was in response to Tylar finding out that her mother had turned her diary over to the police in an attempt to build a case against Steven. They came to their own realization that the only way to save Steven from jail was to murder her mother. There was no way they wouldn't file the charges after all the proof was in the diary. They didn't see another way out.

Steven and Tylar concocted this murder plan, afraid that Steven would be sent to prison for a long time because of the statutory rape charges Joanne had filed against him. They didn't want to risk being separated from each other. They saw the murder and subsequent double suicide as a way of staying together. Just like Romeo and Juliet. What they didn't know was that the statutory rape charges only carried a year worth of prison time, if there was any time at all; it was considered a misdemeanor. Instead of a small charge, with little or no prison time, they exchanged a lifetime of freedom for a lifetime of being locked away due to their irrational nature and horrid actions that were compelled by fear. Neither Tylar, nor Steven were able to determine exactly which one of them came up with the idea of killing Joanne. Tylar had been labeled a liar from the very beginning but all of the evidence they had matched with what Tylar had been saying about that night. Everything fit into place and that's why they believed she was finally telling the truth about Steven.

During Tylar's sentencing the judge addressed her directly, "This was a brutal murder. The court has seen no emotion or even remorse for the loss of your mother...I'm sorry for you Miss Witt, because the person who loved you most and without reservation is gone."

Judi Witt had waited a long time before she would go and visit her granddaughter. When she finally set eyes on Tylar she asked how she could have done such a horrible thing. A look of shock plastered across Tylar's face and she responded, "Do you really think I would have been able to do something like this?" When asked if Judi actually believed her, she responded yes.

Not only did they lose their daughter, Judi and Norb Witt also lost their granddaughter. Judi was able to forgive a little easier than Norb. Norb has since written his granddaughter off for killing his daughter. Her actions were inexcusable. She is not the same little girl that they remembered. They said that the Tylar they knew, wasn't the Tylar that killed Joanne. They choose to remember the little girl that they first visited in the hospital after her birth. Tylar was their third grandchild. They recalled the hospital visit after her birth very fondly. They walked in there with a camera and took many pictures, in awe of their own daughter and their new granddaughter. They choose to remember Tylar as the little girl they had watched grow up, not the monster she had become after killing her own mother, not the girl that constantly defied her own mother and threatened her. Not the girl that wrote in her diary about her dream of finding out her mother had died in a car accident. Tylar had lost her way a long time ago. They choose to only remember the good, but revealed that their family was never going to be the same either. Judi and Norb had come to terms with this.

Norb finally decided to go and see Tylar, after the trial. He had refused to go and see her up until this point. When Norb entered the room, Tylar called him Poppa and embraced him. She began sobbing. Norb held onto her tightly and said, after speaking with her, he could see some kind of remorse for what she had done but he still wasn't in the position of being able to forgive her. "It is hard to forgive someone that helped kill your daughter." Norb and Judi do not visit Tylar in prison, but they do say they write to her very often.

In later interviews Tylar finally began showing small signs of remorse for her mother's brutal ending. At one time Tylar had even considered her mom to be her hero and looked at her as not only a mother figure, but also as a father figure, since she never had a real father. Tylar's personalities were all over the place. She would love her mother one day but threaten to kill her the next.

Steven's mother still holds onto the hope of her son's innocence and the possibility of an appeal. She refuses to believe that the boy she knew would be capable of doing something so unforgivable and so violent to someone else.

The tragic death of Joanne Witt and the story of her daughter and her daughter's boyfriend being the murderers shook the community. A violent history with Joanne and her defiance of any kind of authority figures led Tylar into the arms of someone she felt could protect her. The two scorned lovers had a premeditated and thought out plan to kill the object of their resistance. According to their teenage logic, getting rid of Joanne and committing suicide was the only way they could ever be together. Even the most thought out plans tend to backfire, however, and they were very much alive while Joanne was gone. They traded a life of freedom with some restrictions, for a life spent behind bars. They miscalculated the situation and now live to regret it, day after day, year after year.

WHEN GIRLS NEXT DOOR KILL : THE TRUE STORY OF MELINDA LOVELESS

IRIS OWEN

"Melinda Loveless is the closest thing you will ever look at and know what the devil is. Her eyes are empty. There's nothing inside of her." - Jacqueline Vaught, mother of Shanda Sharer.

BIRTH OF A MONSTER

Melinda Loveless was born on October 28th, 1975 in New Albany, Indiana to Marjorie and Larry Loveless. Melinda would be the youngest of three daughters born to the couple. Her father, Larry, would be a celebrated Vietnam veteran who would be given a hero's welcome in his return home. Behind closed doors, however, Larry was a certified nut who abused his wife and children.

After returning home from military service, Larry would work for the Southern Railroad before becoming a probationary officer with the New Albany Police Department. He would be fired after only eight months on the job after he and his partner would be convicted of assaulting an African-American man.

Larry would justify the assault as he believed that the man slept with his wife.

The incident would be a bit of a head-scratcher as Larry had fantasies of being a cuckold. He would bring his co-workers home to have sex with his wife so he could watch. He would also introduce his wife to a swingers lifestyle.

Larry was a hedonist. He indulged in whatever pleasurable whim his mind could dream up. This also meant spending exorbitant amounts of money. He would buy motorcycles, cars, guns, and other gadgetry. It all became too much as the couple would file for bankruptcy in 1980.

Seeking to turn his family's destiny around, Larry decided they needed religion. He would gather up Melinda and her sisters to attend the Graceland Baptist Church. Both Larry and Margie vowed to stop drinking and put an end to their swinging lifestyles. Larry would soon become a recurring speaker in the church, taking the podium and talking about how Christ had changed his life.

Bad judgment would remain at the forefront of their lives, however. They would let Melinda go with an older man to a hotel room by herself as he claimed he needed to perform an exorcism on her. Larry would become one of the resident family counselors in the church. He would talk to a troubled husband and wife privately and invariably make a pass at the women. He tried to rape one of them and was then excommunicated from the church.

After that incident, Larry decided to turn his back on religion and anything that resembled taking the high road in life. He and his wife would then resume their partying ways with booze and swinging.

CRIMINAL PERVERSIONS

Larry would state that he and his wife had an open relationship. They would enter bars together in Louisville and Larry would pretend to be in the medical field, acting like a big shot doctor or dentist. He would introduce Marjorie as his girlfriend but proceeded to hit on whichever bar girl caught his eye. He would also allow some of his friends from work to have sex with Marjorie but she found his co-workers to be repulsive.

They would have sex orgies with other couples. On one occasion, Margie tried to commit suicide afterward as the experience was so degrading.

Undaunted, Larry would direct a gang rape of Margie and she again tried to kill herself by drowning. She would deny Larry sex for over a month until one night he became so frustrated that he raped her in front of Melinda and her sisters.

Yet she remained with him.

Around 1986, the couple were again in a seedy Louisville bar with Larry chatting up two women. He wanted to take the women home but Margie would not let him. Enraged, Larry would beat his wife up so bad that she was sent to the hospital. He would later be convicted of battery.

By 1988, Larry began working for the United States Postal Service but quit after three months. He loafed around on the job and would often bring undelivered mail back to his home to burn. With little money coming in, visiting extended family would often complain that the Loveless daughters looked undernourished.

INCEST

The rumors about Larry sexually abusing his daughters remain uncorroborated. There were court testimonies that he had fondled Melinda's older sister Michelle when he was a baby. There were also allegations that he molested his wife's thirteen-year-old sister as well as Melinda's cousin for several years.

Melinda's cousin would testify in court that Larry tied all three sisters up in the garage and raped them on by one. Both of Melinda's sisters have said that he molested them but Melinda herself would not admit that it ever happened to her.

She would, however, sleep in bed with him until she was fourteen when he finally left the family.

What is certain was that Larry had a traumatizing effect on all of his daughters. On one occasion, he fired a gun in Michelle's direction when she was only seven, missing intentionally but trying to scare her. He would also take the girls' underwear from the laundry and smell it in front of family members, trying to humiliate them.

Margie would then catch Larry "spying" on a then fifteen-year-old Melinda and her friend. Enraged, she grabbed a knife and began slicing at him. He was able to wrest the knife away from her but had to go to the emergency room for injuries suffered during her attack.

"Margie had an inability to cope," forensic psychologist Paula Orange said. "She tried religion, counseling, hedonism. It all didn't work. Larry was a pervert with a personality disorder. He would run right over Margie and do whatever the hell he wanted. This traumatized Melinda obviously. Her father was abusing her and others while her mother's only response was to try and kill herself."

Margie would try and kill herself one last time but her daughters were able to intervene. Larry would then divorce Margie, wanting to start a new life. He left behind all of his daughters, remarried and moved to Florida.

Melinda took her father's absence the hardest. Larry would humor her for a little while, writing her letters.

Soon the letters stopped and their relationship deteriorated to having no contact.

"The divorce would have a great impact on Melinda," Orange said. "Her home life was horrid, obviously. She had no guidance other than her mother's Christian fundamentalism which would be offset by the way she lived her life. Melinda was raised by spiritual schizophrenics if you will. What she ultimately did was her choice but she did not have any sort of checks and balances in place when she was a child."

Melinda's father, Larry, would be arrested in February of 1993 after open court testimony revealed that he had abused his wife, daughters and their cousin. Because most of the crimes took place between the years of 1968 to 1977, all but one of Larry's charges would be dropped to the statute of limitations in Indiana. He would plead guilty to one count of sexual battery then be released in June of 1995.

He then tried suing the Floyd County Jail system for $39 million dollars. Among his primary complaints during in incarceration was that he was now allowed to sleep during the day or read the newspaper.

His lawsuit was unsuccessful.

THE DOWNWARD SPIRAL

Melinda's behavior became increasingly erratic after her father's rejection. She would get into fights at school and exhibit signs of clinical depression. At the age of fourteen, she entered into a lesbian relationship with a classmate named Amanda Heavrin. Her mother expressed anger at Melinda's sexual orientation but would eventually accept it. Melinda's relationship with Amanda, however, would eventually deteriorate.

The two were not dating when Amanda would become enamored with a younger girl named Shanda Sharer. Melinda would see the two talking outside a school dance and go into a jealous rage.

What she didn't know was that the fifteen-year-old Amanda was smitten with the twelve-year-old Shanda.

Amanda, both looked and dressed like a young boy. She cultivated a "boy band" look and had a sweet disposition that put Shanda's guard down. Shanda was a lonely wallflower at the school. She had recently transferred in and did not have any friends yet. Amanda took advantage of the situation, sending the young girl love notes, flowers and calling her one the phone.

Shanda liked boys but Amanda remained persistent. She knew that Shanda was flattered by the attention and grateful for her company. The new school was a lonely place for the young twelve-year-old.

Their friendship turned into a romance.

And Melinda Loveless could not have that. Amanda was hers and hers alone.

SHANDA SHARER

Shanda and Amanda would spend an increased amount of time together as the school session wore on. When they weren't together, they were writing each other notes or talking on the phone. Shanda's mother, however, caught wind of the relationship and did not approve. She thought Amanda was too old to hang out with Shanda, who was only twelve. The fact that Amanda was a lesbian only raised her eyebrows further.

Shanda was born in Pineville, Kentucky on June 6th, 1979 to Stephen Sharer and Jacqueline Vaught. Her parents would divorce early in her childhood and Shanda would move with her mother to Louisville when she remarried. Shanda would excel in school, receiving good grades while participating in cheerleading, volleyball, and softball. Her mother would divorce again when she was twelve and the family would move to New Albany, Indiana. She would then transfer into a Catholic school after her parents worried about her relationship with Amanda Heavrin. While at Our Lady of Perpetual Help, Shanda played on the basketball team and proceeded to get her life back in order.

"I met her in junior high," Amanda Heavrin recalled. "We became very, very close. We became really good friends."

But Amanda's feelings toward Shanda would only enrage Melinda. Shanda was the passive recipient of Amanda's attention but Melinda didn't see it that way. She would send Shanda notes, one of which read:

Amanda and I are going together and she loves me and I love her and she only wants to be friends with you. You need to accept that! You need to find you a boyfriend because Amanda is mine.

"Shanda would go up to the teacher's desk and Amanda would be staring at her," Melinda said. "I'd see her and Amanda laughing and passing notes and I'd get mad."

The jealousy would eventually come to a head at the school dance. Melinda saw Shanda talking with Amanda outside and immediately confronted her young rival.

"She tried to beat Shanda up," Amanda said. "I got between them and told Shanda to run."

Melinda would be distraught afterward. She began a letter writing campaign to Amanda.

"I want Shanda dead," Melinda wrote.

"I didn't think she was capable of murder," Amanda said. "I thought maybe she'd just try to scare her. Beat her up or something. That's the Melinda I knew. I didn't know her as being a violent person."

TEEN GIRL KILL SQUAD

Melinda wanted Shanda dead.

With murder on her mind, Melinda would enlist the aid of three of her friends. Laurie Tackett, Hope Rippey and Toni Lawrence. Three teenage girls who all had similar, troubled backgrounds. The amount of psychiatric medications prescribed to each of the four teens would be enough to supply a psych ward for a year...and together they would make for an uncontrollable, unpredictable mob.

Together, they would drive over to Shanda's house and listen as Melinda told them of her plan.

But who were these girls that were so easily persuaded to murder?

First, there was Laurie Tackett, born in Madison, Indiana in 1974. She came from a religious family as her mother was a fundamentalist Pentecostal Christian. Taking on extremist views, her mother attempted to strangle Laurie when she found out that she was changing into jeans at school. Her mother also came to Hope Rippey's house unannounced after finding out that Hope's father had given the girl's a Ouija board. She then demanded that the board be set on fire and that Hope's house should be exorcised.

Laurie's father was a convicted felon who worked in a factory. She would later claim she was molested at the ages of five and twelve. Child protective services became involved and would come to Laurie's house unannounced to ensure that she was not being abused.

Laurie would rebel against her parents and would take a profound interest in the occult. She would entertain her friends as she would pretend she was "Deanna the Vampire", acting as if she were possessed.

She would enter into a lesbian relationship at the age of seventeen and her girlfriend would introduce her to self-harm. Her mother would discover her self-mutilating scars and check her into a mental hospital. Laurie would be prescribed anti-depressants upon her release but would slice her wrists again only days later. She would then be diagnosed with borderline personality disorder after a second stint in the psychiatric ward.

Having no goals or concern about the future, Laurie would drop out of high school

An elementary school friend of Laurie, Hope was born in Madison in 1976. Her parents would divorce when she was eight and she would move with her mother and siblings to Quincy, Michigan. Her parents would get back together, however, and the family would return to Madison in 1987. She had grown up with both Laurie and Toni Lawrence and was happy to be reunited with them. Her parents were leery of Laurie, however, and wanted Hope to steer clear from her. Like Laurie, however, Hope was troubled and begin to self-harm at the age of fourteen.

Toni Lawrence rounded out Melinda's trio of killers. She was born in Madison in February of 1976. She would be molested by a relative at age nine and later raped by a teenage boy at age fourteen. The boy would not be charged with the crime, instead, the police only issued a restraining order. Toni would go into therapy after the assault but refused further treatment after a couple of sessions. She would later begin to self-harm as well as sleep around with other boys, getting a reputation as a "whore". She would try to commit suicide in eighth grade.

The stage was set as Melinda had assembled a group of young girls that were just as damaged as she was. Girls that were ticking time bombs. Alone they would have done nothing violent. But together? Together they would be capable of the most horrific crime imaginable.

"Everything that horrible that happened to each of those girls," Shanda Sharer's mother, Jacqueline Vaught said. "Everything that happened to them, they took it out on my child. I think that's what they were doing, I think they just all exploded that night."

The four teenagers drove around the Indiana back roads as Melinda detailed her plan. Laurie was in the driver seat as she was the only one old enough to drive. All piled in, Melinda would tell her acolytes of her plan to scare a girl named Shanda. She pulled out a kitchen knife from her jacket and showed it to the girls.

She's a copycat," Melinda said. "I want to scare her for stealing my girlfriend."

"I'm tired of hearing you just talk about hurting her," Laurie said. "If you really want to hurt her you should go ahead and really do it."

Melinda took the challenge. She needed a volunteer to lure Shanda out of the home. She knew that Shanda's parents were no longer allowing her to see Amanda anymore. But if they could use Amanda as bait, they could lure her out.

Melinda knew Shanda's address but the girls got lost a few times and stopped to ask for directions.

Finally arriving at the home, Melinda sent Hope Rippey to the door.

Jacqueline Vaught came to the door and saw Hope in front of her. She had never seen the teen before but didn't think anything wrong when Hope politely asked if Shanda was home.

"Shanda had never been anywhere where we didn't know where she was or who she was with," Vaught said. "Shanda was not allowed to go to anybody's house where I didn't call the parents that I didn't go there. I was very, very protective."

She called Shanda down and left the teen girls alone.

"Your friend Amanda is upset and really needs to talk with you," Hope said.

"Why?" Shanda whispered, looking back to make sure her mother wasn't listening. She was no longer allowed to have anything to do with Amanda.

"She's waiting for you at the Witches Castle."

Shanda knew that Hope was referring to an old, stone house, located on an isolated hill next to the Ohio River. It was a creepy but teens like to hang out there.

"I'm having nothing more to do with Amanda."

"Have a heart," Hope said. "You must care about her, couldn't you be there for her just one last time?"

"Why did Amanda send you instead of coming herself?"

"Amanda knew she couldn't come to your house."

"I can't go now," Shanda said, looking behind herself again. "My parents are up. I'll sneak out around midnight if you want to come back hen."

Hope agreed and returned the car without Shanda.

Melinda immediately confronted Hope on why she didn't have Shanda with her. Hope explained that Shanda agreed that if they came back at midnight, she'd be willing to come with them.

The teens then head out to a nearby punk rock concert. Both Toni and Hope get bored and have sex with two boys they've just met to pass the time.

Midnight rolled back around and the girls returned to Shanda's home.

"I can't wait to kill Shanda," Melinda said. "I'd like to fuck her."

Melinda then hid in the back seat. The other girls covered with a jacket and trash from inside the car.

Hope then went and got Shanda.

"They were not mean looking, dirty child molesters," Shanda's mother, Jacqueline Vaught said. They were two children that looked like her. They said just walk twenty-five feet and talk to her. And that's what she did."

Shanda squeezed into the front seat, sitting in between Laurie and Toni. The girls pretended to like Shanda at first but soon she began feeling uncomfortable.

"The Witches Castle is a short drive away," Laurie said. "You know the legend? That house had once been owned by nine witches who had controlled the town and the townspeople had burnt the house to get rid of the witches."

"So what's up with you and Amanda?" Hope asked, turning to Shanda.

"We'd been going out for quite awhile," Shanda said. "I really cared about her."

"I see."

"What's wrong with Amanda?" Shanda asked. "Why does she have to see me so badly?"

"Surprise!" Melinda screamed, jumping out from the backseat. She grabbed Shanda's hair, pulled her head back and put the knife to the young girl's throat.

"Please don't hurt me," Shanda said.

The girls all laughed.

Laurie stepped on the gas...

CRUEL AND SADISTIC

"Bitch," Melinda hissed as she pressed the knife down on Shanda's throat. "Don't move, don't make a sound."

They arrived at the Witches Castle, parked and pulled Shanda inside. Melinda tied up Shanda's hands with a rope. Hope waved the knife in front of Shanda's face, taunting her. Laurie took along an old t-shirt and set it on fire.

"You see that?" Laurie held up the burning shirt before the crying Shanda. "That's what you're going to look like before the night is over!"

Melinda then ripped off Shanda's necklace and bracelets. She handed them to Toni and they took turns admiring the items. Hope ripped off the Mickey Mouse Musical watch from Shanda's wrist and put it in her pocket.

Several cars passed before the castle and then the girls went quiet, waiting for the coast to clear. Not satisfied that they would have total privacy, the girls dragged Shanda back to the car and stuffed her in the back seat, covering her with a blanket.

Laurie made a pit stop at a gas station while Melinda stood guard over Shanda. Hope went inside to pay for the gas while Toni makes a phone call.

She does not tell the person she is calling about the kidnapping or ask for help.

The girls then go back to their hometown of Madison, Indiana, an hour away.

Once there, they drove a few miles past Laurie's home and pull off into a seldom used logging road. Laurie stops the car and they all get out. Hope and Toni complain about the cold and wait inside the vehicle.

Melinda then hauled out Shanda from the back seat. The girl resisted until Laurie came to help and they muscle her out of the vehicle, throwing her to the ground.

"Take your clothes off, bitch," Melinda screamed.

Crying, Shanda complied with the request. Hope and Toni watch from the car window.

Melinda then took Shanda's clothes and threw them into the back seat. "I want them as souvenirs.

Playing along, Hope put on Shanda's polka dot bra. Toni turned on the radio.

"Shanda had hugged me," Laurie said in a December 1992 interview. "She asked me not to let Melinda do it. She was crying. There wasn't anything I could do."

Laura instead held Shanda's hands behind her back. Melinda then began punching the little girl.

"Please let me go," Shanda screamed. "I'll stay away from Amanda."

"Shut up!" Melinda punched Shanda hard in the stomach. She followed this up by pulling her by the hair as she fell to the ground. Shanda was prone and Michelle repeatedly kneed her in the mouth

Shanda winced and yelped in pain.

Her adrenaline and nerve increasing, Melinda took out her knife and tried to cut Shanda's throat. The blade is too dull, however.

"Get over here, Hope!" Melinda commanded.

Hope obeyed and Melinda ordered her to help hold Shanda down. Melinda then tried to use her foot to pierce the knife through Shanda's throat.

The girls then took turns stabbing Shanda in the chest.

The knife was still too dull.

"We need to just strangle her," Laura said, taking the rope and wrapping around her neck.

"Please don't kill me," Shanda pleaded.

Melinda just laughed. She sat on her Shanda's legs as Laura straddled her chest, tightening the rope.

Shanda would pass out and the girls thought she died. They picked up her body and tossed her in the trunk of the car.

POINT OF NO RETURN

The girls would arrive at Laura's home, triumphant. They would go upstairs to Laura's bedroom and drink soda. Laura, the occult aficionado, would take out her "runes stones" and perform a "future reading" for the girls.

"Our futures look good," Laurie said until they heard her dog barking outside. The teens rushed to the window and listened. They could hear Shanda screaming from the trunk of the car.

Laura went to the kitchen and got a paring knife. She hurried outside, opened the trunk and began stabbing Shanda repeatedly. The girl quieted down and Laurie closed the trunk again.

Laurie returned to her bedroom, covered in blood. She washed herself up and then addressed the kill squad with a renewed need for cruelty.

"We have to go for a ride," Laurie said.

"I'm tired," Toni said.

"Me too," Hope agreed.

Melinda and Laurie dismissed the girls and went for a drive by themselves. They headed back to the isolated road, parked and then went to check of Shanda had died yet.

The little girl sat up. Her eyes rolled in the back of her head. She tried to speak but was only to say one word.

"Mommy."

AN ENDLESS NIGHT OF TORTURE

Laurie picked up a tire iron from the trunk and bashed Shanda across the head. She closed the trunk again and they drove along the back roads. The mood turned somber and silent until they once again head Shanda choking in the back trunk.

Laura stopped and got again, opening the trunk and bashing Shanda in the head the tire iron once more. This time, a chunk of flesh from Shanda's temple went flying into the night air.

Laurie came back to the car, blood splattered across her arms.

"She looked as though she was painted red," Laurie laughed, waving the bloody tire iron and under Melinda's nose who smelled it with glee.

Melinda and Laurie then go back to Laurie's home. The woke up Toni and Hope, laughing and filling them in on how much further they tortured Shanda. The foursome discussed what they should do with the body until Laurie's mother woke up.

She berated her daughter for being out so late then yelled at her even more for having her friends spend the night without asking.

After her mother's lecture ended, Laurie led the girls to the back of her house.

ONE LAST ACT OF EVIL

"There's a burn pile out here ," Laura said, skipping through the woods beyond her back yard. They would find the burn pile but it would be covered in frost.

"That won't work," Laura said. "We're going to need some gasoline."

The girls went back to the car and opened the trunk, needing another look at their victim.

Toni refused to look at the tortured body of Shanda, shocked by the amount of blood covering the girl.

"Start the car and rev the engine if she starts screaming," Laurie said.

Hope grabbed a bottle of Windex in the trunk and began spraying Shanda's body.

"You're not looking so hot are you?" Hope taunted.

Shanda was semi-conscious. She sat up, her naked body covered in dried blood.

"Laurie!" Laurie's mother called out.

"Shit," Laurie slammed the trunk lid on Shanda's head and went to find out what her mother wanted.

After a few minutes, Laurie returned and the girls drove to a gas station. Laurie ordered Toni to buy a two liter Pepsi bottle from inside. She came back and Laurie emptied the bottle into the dirt then filled it with gasoline.

"We could get rid of her out by Lemon Road," Hope offered.

Laurie followed Hope's directions, driving onto the old country logging road. Toni would remain in the car as the three other girls pulled Shanda out from the vehicle.

Hope would pour the Pepsi bottle filled with gas over Shanda. Laura lit a match and tossed it on the body.

The fire blew high. The girls giggled and ran back to the car, speeding away.

"Wait," Melinda said. "Turn the car back around."

"The way it was told to me," retired detective Steve Henry said. "Was that they drove away and turned around and came back past the body thinking that she would be burned completely up and there would be no trace of her and she was still there so Melinda set her on fire again."

Laurie complied, doubling back and stopping in front of the burning body. They watched for a few minutes until Melinda stepped out of the vehicle with the Pepsi bottle.

She looked down on Shanda, her body in a fetal position. Tongue lolling in and out of her mouth as she convulsed in pain.

Melinda poured the remainder of the gas on Shanda and tossed another match on the little girl.

The teens then drove off and ate breakfast at a McDonald's.

"What does this remind you of?" Laurie asked as she held up a piece of sausage.

"Shanda's body," Melinda laughed. "Burned to a crisp."

Shanda was not dead yet, however. Soot was later found in her airways which meant that she was burning in the fumes around her. She was conscious while they set her on fire.

"They didn't know how to tell me how she died," Shonda's mother, Jacqueline Vaught said. "And I saw it on television. That she'd been burned alive. I didn't know that."

Melinda would then call her ex-girlfriend, Amanda Heavrin and confess to the crime.

"She told me everything that happened," Amanda recalled. "I thought it was a joke. Because I just cannot fathom that four little girls would do this to another human being. This is stuff you wouldn't even do to an animal."

She thought that if she removed the competition that she could have Amanda.

CONFESSION AND TRIAL

Toni Lawrence would be the girl to come forward and confess. She came home hysterical, telling her parents what happened. They took her down to the police station and she told detectives what happened.

All four teenagers would be charged as adults. This forced them to accept plea bargains as they wanted to avoid the death penalty.

The defense played on the fact that all four girls were victims of physical and/or sexual abuse in their childhood. Hope, Toni, and Laurie had histories of self-harming behavior. Laurie was clinically diagnosed with a borderline personality disorder and had both visual and auditory hallucinations.

Toni would cooperate in exchange for a lesser sentence. She was allowed to plead guilty to one count of criminal confinement which got her a maximum sentence of twenty years. Hope would be sentenced to sixty years with ten years suspended for mitigating circumstances plus ten years of medium-supervision probation. She would continue to appeal and the judge would reduce the sentence to thirty-five years. Both Laurie and Melinda wold be sentenced to sixty years and sent to the Indiana Women's Prison in Indianapolis.

Melinda's attorney would appeal for her release in October of 2007. He would argue that Melinda had been "profoundly retarded" by the abuse she suffered during childhood. He further argued hat she had not been competently represented during her initial sentencing. He also played the "age card", as Melinda was only sixteen years old when she entered the plea agreement with the state of Indiana and needed consent from a parent or guardian.

The appeal for her release was denied but the sentencing was reduced down to make her eligible for parole in fifteen years. It is becoming apparent that Melinda and Laurie could be released from prison as early as 2022.

Toni would be released from jail in December of 2000 after serving nine years. She would remain on parole until 2002. Hope was released from the Indiana Women's Prison on April 28, 2006, serving for fourteen years.

"None of these girls were born murderers," Vaught said. "They weren't born to murder children. They weren't born to be in prison. This what we do as parents. We mold our children into what they are."

Shanda's father, Stephen, would die at the age of 53 due to alcoholism. Stephen had become depressed over the death of his daughter and subsequently "drank himself to death" over the years.

"Steve could not have been a prouder father," Vaught said. "Shanda was his life. From the day that she died he did everything he could to kill himself beside put a gun to his head. And finally he drank himself to death and he died at fifty-three."

"Melinda has cheated me out of being with my daughter during this life. It is my wish for you (Melinda) that you live your life with memories of her screams and sign of her burned and mutilated body. I hope and pray you remember these words for the rest of your life: May you rot in hell."

WHEN GIRLS NEXT DOOR KILL : THE TRUE STORY OF CINDY COLLIER & SHIRLEY WOLF

IRIS OWEN

"Today, Cindy and I ran away and killed an old lady. It was lots of fun" -
Shirley Wolf's journal, June 14th, 1983.

Shirley Wolf and Cindy Collier met in a juvenile detention center and had known each other for only a few hours when they decided to escape and randomly kill a stranger.

They would go to a senior condominium center in Auburn, California where they would seek an elderly victim.

They would find one in the eighty-five-year-old Anna Brackett. They entered her home under the ruse that they needed to use the phone to call their parents.

The girls would brutally murder the elderly woman in a crime so shocking that deputy sheriffs were initially in denial that two young girls would commit such a crime.

But how did they get to the point mentally where they could commit such a horrid act? This is the story of how they got there.

EARLY LIFE

Cindy Collier wasn't the nice girl next door. Her entire body language spoke of rage and hostility. By the age of twelve, she was a regular at the juvenile hall where she would routinely assaulting staff and inmate alike.

Incorrigible, she had been arrested for burglary, theft and drug possession.

Because of her age, Cindy was often spared jail time and was sentenced to community service. She would most often be sent to pick up litter on highways but the punishment wasn't enough to deter her from a life of crime.

"She was a smart ass towards everyone," former classmate Mike Fluty said.

No one was spared her rage. At fourteen years old, she had no problem harassing adults as well, randomly accosting people on the street.

"What are you looking at?" she asked a woman walking by as she smoked a cigarette. "You think you're better than me?"

She would then raise her fist to the woman and force her to run away. "Oooh!" Cindy taunted. "Ooooh! Come on, you want some?"

"Cindy liked to intimidate," forensic psychologist Paula Orange said. "She had learned it was better to be a predator than the prey very early on in life. Her early childhood would shape the monster she would become."

Cindy's parents divorced when she was one year old. Her mother would remarry but that would end in divorce as well. She would take care of Cindy and her three sons during the day and go to a waitress job at night.

Cindy stated that she had been raped by an undisclosed family member and by another man who threw her down a flight of stairs after he finished with her.

"Her mother reportedly had different children all by different men," Orange said. "Cindy was molested by one of her mother's endless string of men that she brought into the home."

Cindy would talk about her "rotten" childhood and describe being "raped a few times." She tried to commit suicide on several occasions but that only brought her more frustrations. So instead of harming herself, she decided she would harm others.

"I want them to pay," she said.

By the time she entered Chana High in Auburn, California, Cindy had a well-established reputation of someone who should be feared. Using physical intimidation, she would randomly choose a girl she didn't like and the bullying would begin. She would push and yell, getting in their face. Her victims would be spared no quarter, on one occasion, Cindy ripped the blouse of a girl and forced her to run down the street topless.

"She was a trained bully," Orange said. "She knew exactly how to push the buttons of her victims, strip them of their dignity. It was done to her at home so it was easy for her to pass along the abuse."

Cindy was a menacing presence on campus to the other petite girls. At 5'9" and 140 pounds, she could beat up any girl in the school. She had a strong jawline and broad shoulders but it was her eyes that set her apart from the average bully. Eyes that pierced through her victims and gave them an implicit message.

I want to kill you.

Cindy's crimes would not be limited to physical assaults. She would grab and take whatever she wanted. She would go into liquor stores, stuff food into her pockets and leave. She would go into malls and steal cassette tapes at the record store. After a few months, she graduated to stealing a car. This would land her in a juvenile detention center where she would be a kindred spirit unlike any other she had met before.

LIKE LOOKING INTO A MIRROR

Like Cindy, Shirley Wolf had been the victim of sexual abuse. Her father, Louis Wolf, would rape her. But the abuse didn't stop with just her father. She was a molested by her paternal grandfather and uncle as well.

An observant kindergarten teacher noticed the odd behavior of Shirley and recommended that she get psychiatric help to no avail.

Shirley didn't know where else to turn as she would be abused by all of the men in her life. At the age of six years old, she had run away for the first time. The streets were too rough for her, however, and she was scared back home by the dark characters of Brooklyn.

A lost little girl with nowhere else to go but the house where she was abused.

Her father, Louis, worked as a carpenter but suffered an accident that forced him to take disability. He would remain at home and begin bossing his children around. Then it turned to the sexual abuse of his daughter, Shirley.

When Shirley was around six, the family would move from the east coast to Placerville, California so Louis could be closer to his own family.

Louis Wolf would send Shirley's mother Katherine on an errand to get some groceries one morning. He then locked Shirley's three younger brothers out of the house and turned his attention to Shirley.

He cornered her in the bathroom and raped her.

Shirley would never forgive her father for what he did to her.

Louis would rape his daughter sometimes as much as three times per day. By the time she reached puberty, he put her on birth control.

Shirley never told her mother because she didn't want to break up the family.

Louis would tell Shirley to not tell her mother what he had done. Shirley obliged only because she was afraid how badly the news would hurt her mother.

Eventually, however, the abuse became so intolerable that she told her mother.

Her mother suspected it all along. She then went to the authorities.

Louis would deny that he molested Shirley but plead guilty to reduced charges which brought his sentencing down to a mere one-hundred days.

Louis was told that if he fought the charges, he would be facing fifty years. So he took the three months.

Shirley would then be removed from the home which was her worst fear. She would be bounced from foster home to foster home where she told of feeling "like a stranger."

"You get to the point where you're pushed in a corner and I just came back fighting," Shirley said. "I want to go home. I forgive my father and I try to forget it. He's apologized to me, my family and to God."

A MATCH TO A FLAME

It would be only fitting that the first time the girls would meet, it would be under the guise of violence.

At the detention center, Shirley was being beaten to a pulp by a fellow inmate in the hallway. As per usual, no guards were around. But Cindy stood her ground against the bigger girl, to no avail.

The girl threw her against the wall, punched her in the stomach and twisted her arm.

"Who are you?" Cindy asked as she came upon the two girls fighting.

"Shirley Wolf."

"I like you, Shirley Wolf."

And with that, Cindy got her opponent into a full nelson, easily overpowering Shirley's tormentor.

"Let her have it," Cindy said.

Shirley didn't hesitate. She began pummeling the girl, all of the rage of being abused all of her life came forth as she gave the girl a beat-down.

Cindy threw the girl to the ground and the two laughed as she moaned in pain.

"Later loser," Shirley sniffed.

Cindy laughed. The girl had spunk and they spent the next couple of hours exchanging their life stories.

For some reason, Cindy did not feel hatred toward Shirley. She felt like they had an unspoken bond but she didn't know why.

The truth was, they were both ticking time bombs.

"I think it was an unfortunate chemistry between the two girls," Shirley's defense attorney Thomas Condit said. "I think it also had to do with finding a new friend and wanting to show that she was capable of doing anything that the friend was."

Shirley was the opposite of Cindy in one regard, however, as she did not have Cindy's assurance. Shirley felt "hopeless and helpless" as she talked about running away from the detention center. She talked about this as if it were an impossibility, a faraway dream.

But Cindy felt otherwise. She behaved as if she knew all the answers.

"I can get us out of here," Cindy said with total assurance.

"You can?"

"Sure. I do it all the time. But we're going to need a car. This place where I used to live as all kinds of old people. We can steal one of their cars. But we'll probably have to kill them."

"Yeah," Shirley said.

"You know," Cindy said. "In case one of them rats us out."

Cindy led the way as the girls escaped. They talked about how they would put their sadistic plan in motion. They wanted to find someone old and feeble...someone who could not fight back...someone who they could kill for fun.

"I suppose a good analogy would be to compare the girls to the boys from Columbine who would come over a decade later," Orange said. "One needed the other to pull off such a horrid act. They needed that voice over their shoulder to egg them on. They both wanted the same thing and together they could make it happen."

Both Cindy and Shirley would dye their hair red in order to disguise themselves. They then went "victim hunting," touring Cindy's old neighborhood in Auburn Green, a condo for senior citizens. They wanted a car. A nice one. So they began searching the parking lot for a car and would match the number on the parking slot to the condo number.

Then they would knock on the door. Their questions were innocent. They would ask for directions, a glass of water or ask to use the phone. But there was something about their demeanor, a sinister or insincere look in their eye that set off the alarm bells for all of the senior citizens they met. They were allowed inside by Joe Becker and his wife who gave them a glass of water. When they left, however, the elderly couple immediately washed the glass and scrubbed the phone with alcohol, the girls seemed so dirty.

"They were looking for an easy target," Orange said. "Becker was seventy but still probably too much of a hassle for them. They needed easy."

Then they knocked on the door of Anna Brackett.

"We decided we were going to kill her when we saw her," Shirley said. "She was just an old lady. Just a perfect setup. We killed her because we wanted her car and we didn't want to get caught."

Anna was a retired seamstress who worked for Sears. She had great-grandchildren who were the ages of Cindy and Shirley.

She was a helpful and kind person to all her knew her. She didn't hesitate in helping some girls that were the ages of her great-grandchildren.

"Can I help you?" Anna opened the door with a smile.

"Hi," Cindy said. "Can you please help us? We need to call our parents and the phone down the street is not working."

"Sure," Anna said, opening up her door.

Ann was congenial and didn't see any reason not to trust the girls. She let them into her home and the threesome chatted for over an hour. They sat on the couch and she gave them soda. She would show the girls pictures of her family. Pictures of her children, grandchildren.

"It is unusual for a sociopath to want to know about their victim," Orange said. "They really don't want to know their victim because it humanizes them. So perhaps the teen girls were hesitant at first. But it was more of a case of them working up the nerve to do what they set out to do."

The phone rang and Anna went up to answer it.

The call came from her son.

"I'm on my way," her son said.

"Okay," Anna said, hanging up the phone. "I'm sorry, girls. My son is coming to pick me up. We're going to the bingo parlor."

"Now," Cindy said as the girls pounced.

Shirley grabbed the elderly woman by the throat and slammed her to the ground.

"What are you doing?" Anna screamed. "What are you doing?"

Cindy sprinted to the kitchen and rifled through the drawers. She found a butcher knife and gave it to Shirley.

"Do it," Cindy commanded.

Shirley would then stab the helpless old woman without mercy. She would recall stabbing her in the neck and "freaking out" because the old lady kept screaming.

"You're killing me!" Anna shouted.

"Good," Shirley said, slicing the knife down again. She would stop only when she saw the blood coming out of Anna's mouth.

Anna Brackett would suffer over twenty-eight stab wounds although the coroner believed it could have been more as the blade went through the same entry point. There was one stab wound where the blade had gone in four inches deep past Anna's breastplate.

"She died a horrific death," Orange said. "Painful and horrific. I've read some psychiatrists say that Shirley was getting revenge on all of the people that hurt her in the past, that in some way Anna symbolized her mother and she was killing her mother symbolically. I believe that is psychobabble. Shirley was not that bright. She was following the lead of Cindy and they wanted to kill and maim. That was the point. Not to subconsciously work out her anger. She was a defective unit."

Cindy then sifted through all of Anna's drawers and closets looking for money. They found the keys to the old woman's 1970 Dodge and ripped the two telephones from the wall.

They went into the garage and found out that the keys they had stolen would not start the car. Angered, they left the condo on foot and began hitch-hiking.

Ironically, Anna's son Carl would drive pass them on the street, ignoring the girls who had their thumbs out.

He then entered his mother's home and discovered her mutilated body on the floor.

It was a surreal scene for her son. His mother on the floor in a pool of blood. Trapped in his own real life horror movie, Carl would never have guessed that two underage girls would be capable of such a thing.

LIKE A DAY AT THE OFFICE

Cindy and Shirley made it to her home in Auburn. They turned on the television, eagerly awaiting news of the murder they had committed.

Too many people had spotted them around the neighborhood. In all, eleven people informed the investigating officers of the two red-headed girls with the strange demeanor.

Some remembered Cindy from when she lived with her grandparents in the condo development. The deputies, however, didn't believe that two teenage girls could have done what they did to Anna.

Back home, the girls would cheer as their murder was reported on the evening news.

Then they went to sleep.

At 2:30 a.m the deputies would arrive at the house of Cindy Collier.

Deputy George Coelho didn't believe the girls did the crime. But after a few minutes of questioning, Shirley confessed.

Cindy, however , would not only confess to the crime, she would gloat.

"She started to laugh," Deputy Coelho said.

Cindy expressed little remorse. She told the deputies that she felt like killing more people.

Shirley was excited and giddy as they had done something that "they had never done before."

They were placed under arrest and one of the deputies began reading her the Miranda rights. Shirley interrupted him, repeating the rights verbatim as she was already familiar with the process.

Cindy would tell the police that she felt jealousy toward anyone who appeared happy and normal. She felt such envy that she wanted to kill them.

The deputy expressed shock as Cindy detailed her desires of wanting to hurt people. She bragged about stabbing, shooting and throwing people into the Auburn Damn. The officers knew it was all bravado...with the exception of what they did to Ann Brackett.

The two girls would go to trial in July of 1983...a juvenile court.

What the girls wanted was fame and publicity.

They would get it as the brutal murder would be talked about in numerous high-profile magazines and the court case would reach a national audience. A movie called "Fun" was produced, chronicling the girl's first day together.

CRIME AND PUNISHMENT

Shirley's attorney, Thomas Condit, would enter a plea of not guilty by reason of insanity. "I'd like to say that Shirley felt sorry," Condit said. "But I can't. That's part of her problem. She told me that while she was killing the old lady, she was thinking of everybody she hated—her father and his mother. But the psychiatrist believes it was a symbolic killing of her own mother."

Both girls would receive the maximum imprisonment for underage girls. They would remain in jail until the age of twenty-five then be released.

"Shirley really can't understand the difference between right and wrong," Condit said. "How do you appreciate right and wrong when you have a father telling you it's wrong not to stay home and service him when you should be in school?"

THE AFTERMATH

Cindy would spend the next nine years at the California Youth Authority facility in Ventura. She would obtain an associate of arts degree then go on to study law at Pepperdine University. She would go on to have four children and live in Northern California without any further brushes with the law.

Shirley would be sent to the Central California Women's Facility near Chowchilla.

She would threaten other inmates and her jailers during her time in prison. She spent her days reading romance novels as she tries to take her mind off the tormented childhood which led her to be capable of such a crime.

"I think of my dad and it hurts," Shirley said. "I'll just feel pain and I'll have to cry to get it out. I can't really pinpoint where it's from. God knows, I'll get hurt and just cry."

Shirley would complete her high school education and become a born-again Christian. The attempts to improve her life would prove futile, however.

She had tried to contact her parents but they never returned her calls or letters. Finally, in the summer of 1992, Shirley tracked down the number of her parents in the Pacific Northwest. Louis, the man who had molested her, would answer her call.

They had not spoken in four years but he had told her that her mother had left him a few months prior, leaving the three young boys with him. Shirley asked about her favorite brother, L.J., but her father avoided giving her a straight answer.

Shirley wanted desperately to know what happened to her younger brother but could not locate him anywhere. Her father would then stop returning her calls.

On June 30th, 1995, Shirley would be freed from prison after serving twelve years for the murder of Anna Brackett.

Her father would die in 2002.

Unlike Cindy, Shirley's life of petty crimes would continue. She would get involved in prostitution, theft, and burglaries. She has shown remorse for the murder but also stated that "there is no going back."

Both women are now free, getting leniency for the crime because of their age. Their light sentences would draw the ire of Anna's son, Carl, who would rage at the judicial system that gave his mother no justice.

KILLER TEEN : THE TRUE STORY OF KRISTINA FETTERS

JANET NIXON

Kristina Fetters was the youngest woman in the state of Iowa to get sentenced to life in prison without parole after she murdered her great-aunt. But eighteen years later she would be re-sentenced after the Supreme Court ruled that mandatory life sentences for minors was unconstitutional.

Kristina would later be released to a hospice center as she developed breast cancer in prison.

But what happened that fateful night of October 25th, 1994? Kristina was only fourteen years old, five-feet tall and barely one hundred pounds. Yet she committed one of the most brutal assaults in the history of her Iowa town.

This is what transpired in her life before and after she committed a brutal murder of her loving aunt.

EARLY LIFE

She was born Kristina Joy Fetters on February 5th, 1980. The product of a biracial union between her mother Darlene and an African-American man, Kristina did not get to know her father growing up.

Instead, she spent her childhood with Arlene and Wayne Klehm. They were the great-aunt and great-uncle of Kristina but she thought of them as her grandparents. She would refer to Wayne as "Uncle Sheenie" and to her aunt Arlene as "Pooper."

Kristina would play at their home as a young child, swinging from bedsheets tied to a tree in the front yard of the couple's one story home.

Wayne was the easy going one of the couple. Arlene, on the other hand, was the one who enforced discipline on the precocious Kristina.

But Kristina was close to her aunt as were all of her other cousins. Arlene was described as a 'spitfire', a woman who spoke her mind.

"Arlene was just a tiny framed, little woman that would tell you exactly where to go and how you could get there," Kristina's cousin Shanna Sickles said.

Kristina would not meet her biological father until she turned eight years old. She wanted a close relationship with him but the bond never materialized.

"I want him in my life," Kristina said to the Iowa Register in 1996. "I need him in my life. I don't think he knows what he wants."

RUNNING WITH A BAD CROWD

Kristina seemed to have little guidance in her early life. At only twelve-years old, she would meet a twenty-three year old African-American man from Milwaukee named Anthony Leon Hoover. He was a gangster "wannabe", seeking membership into a street gang called the "Black Gangster Disciples." Immature and naïve to the perils of the street, Kristina told the man that she was seventeen years old and ran away with him.

But in June of 1993, Hoover would be arrested on kidnapping charges. He held Kristina at gunpoint, broke her nose and then raped her.

Kristina could not cope with the trauma inflicted by the older man. She would not go to school and would runaway on a weekly basis.

By January of 1994, she was so troubled that she was sent to the Orchard Place, an unlocked facility for minors with behavioral problems. Kristin was placed on Prozac and underwent treatment.

"She was on three different medications that are well known to not play well together now," her friend Jaimi Ross said. "She was showing every warning sign, every red flag that you possibly could on these drugs and they were all ignored."

She also sought solace in Christianity to no avail. A Polk County Juvenile Court officer said that Kristina "lived in a fantasy world most of the time."

Her mother, Denise, would support this assessment as she described her daughter as having hallucinatory episodes.

"She'd say 'look, look, there's Johnny. He's laying on the floor," Denise said. "There's a knife in his head. He's bleeding. Somebody help him, somebody help him. And the teachers would try and re-direct her, you know, you need to get up here and finish your homework."

In September of 1994, her Uncle Wayne would die. Aunt Arlene then sent her grand-niece a handwritten letter, trying to smooth things over.

"Let's be nice to each other and forgive me if I hurt you," Arlene Klehm stated in the letter.

But Kristina would not take the olive branch of her great-aunt.

PLOTTING A MURDER

Ten months later, on October 25th, 1994, Kristina and her roommate Jeanie Fox escaped from the Orchard Place.

Their destination was Kristina's great-aunt's home in Polk County, Iowa.

Arlene Klehm was 76-years old and had little contact with her grand-niece since her placement into the mental health facility.

Living in her fantasy world, Kristina concocted the idea that her aunt Arlene had a lot of money. She planned to escape from the facility, kill her aunt and ride off into the sunset in her truck. What her plans were beyond that, she didn't know.

All she knew was that she needed a partner in crime.

First, she approached a girl named Jessica Wilhite. She explained that her aunt had a lot of money and it would be an easy kill. They could take both her money and her truck after doing the deed.

Jessica remained non-committal.

Kristina then went to Tisha Versendaal and told her of her plan.

"She sits in a chair all day," Kristina said. "I'll stab her then cut her throat. She keeps her money in a safe. We'll take all her money then get away in her truck."

But she found no taker in Tish who was due to leave the facility soon. Instead, she settled on Jeanie Fox, who wanted out of the facility.

Telling Jeanie her plan of escaping and leaving the part of killing her aunt out of the equation, the two packed their bags. They left the facility without incident and that is when Kristina told Jeanie of her other plans.

"Do you want to come with me to kill my aunt?" Kristina asked.

A FIELD TRIP TO MURDER

The girls stopped at three different homes before heading off to kill her aunt. The final stop was at the apartment of a friend where Kristina got a small paring knife.

"What do you need that for?" the friend asked.

"I'm going to kill my aunt," Kristina laughed as she left the apartment.

The two girls arrived at Klehm's home and noticed that a van was parked outside.

Her aunt was entertaining company.

Kristina wanted to wait as she didn't want any witnesses.

The two girls then knelt behind a fence and waited for her aunt's friends to leave.

"I am going to fucking kill her," Kristina repeated the sentence like a mantra outside the home. "Satan has given me the power to do so."

Her aunt's visitors finally left and the two impatient girls knocked on the door. The old woman let them both in, unsuspecting of what the girls had in store for her.

The three small-talked in the kitchen before Kristina pulled Jeanie into a side room.

"I'm going to fucking kill her," Kristina said, again like a mantra as if she were psyching herself up.

Gathering up the nerve, Kristina marched into the kitchen where her aunt was sitting and smashed her over the head with a tea kettle.

Arlene fell to the ground. She tried to get up, woozy, and asked what happened.

Kristina showed no mercy. She exchanged the kettle for a heavy metal skillet and smashed it across her aunt's head.

"Give me the knife," Kristina called out to Jeanie.

Taking the paring knife, Kristina tried to slice Arlene's throat but the knife wasn't sharp enough. She then rummaged through the kitchen drawers, found a larger knife and stabbed her aunt in the back.

"Anthony!" Kristina cried out with every stab (according to Jeanie). "Anthony! Anthony!"

"Help!" Arlene wailed at Jeanie who stood and watched. The bloodied woman wobbled over to the phone but Kristina got there first.

"No!" the teen girl said, ripping the phone off the hook.

Kristina would stab her aunt a total of five times in the back. There were also defensive wounds on her hand and lumps on her head.

Her aunt now dead, Kristina wanted a change of clothes. But first she rummaged through Arlene's bedroom, stealing her necklaces and other small pieces of jewelry.

"We need to find her damn keys," Kristina called out to Jeanie.

They searched for the keys to both the safe and the truck to no avail.

Kristina then thought she heard police sirens in the distance. The two girls began to run and Kristina started to cry.

The girls ran down the block, pounding on the doors of neighbors until police arrived.

"I killed my aunt," Kristina sobbed. "I killed my aunt."

"It was a grisly scene," Detective Neil Schwartz recalled as he came upon Arlene's body. "Brutal. Very bloody."

THE AFTERMATH

Kristina would be charged with first-degree murder and her case was transferred from the juvenile system to a district court in order for her to be tried as an adult.

Her defense team would enter a plea of insanity. She would undergo psychiatric examination with Dr. Michael Taylor who stated that he didn't think Kristina was insane but rather had a personality disorder.

Her planning was too precise and her deception upon entering her aunt's house did not suggest that she was insane, the doctor explained. Furthermore, she understood what she had done after the killing.

But another psychiatrist, Dr. Gaylord Nordine, believed that Kristina was in a psychotic state caused by the Prozac. Dr. Taylor disagreed, stating that Prozac would not have had any adverse consequences on her and that Kristina was also on Thorazine at the time which should have made more her even more docile.

"In talking with her I found absolutely no evidence of any type of psychiatric disorder, " Taylor said. "And in talking with her I found absolutely no indication that she was doing anything on October 25, 1994, other than killing her aunt."

On December 18th, 1995, Kristina would be sentenced to life in prison without parole.

She would serve out her sentence at the Iowa Correctional Institution for Women in Mitchellville, Iowa. She would file appeal after appeal as her attorneys would bring up the fact that this was cruel and unusual punishment for a juvenile.

According to her friends, Kristina didn't forgive herself for what she had done.

"When everybody else was telling her that they forgave her and they're showing her unconditional love," Jaimi Ross said. "She didn't feel she deserved it. It was very hard for her to accept."

Kristina and Jaimi would becoming close friends in jail. They had to...They were two children in an adult prison who were serving life sentences.

When other children came into the facility, Kristina and Jaimi would serve as mentors of sorts.

"They came in and everybody would share their story. It would be Kristina, myself, and another inmate. We'd just open ourselves up and let it all pour out and let them see us for the same flawed humans that they are."

A TERMINAL ILLNESS

In 2013, however, Kristina would be diagnosed with inoperable breast cancer. By November of that year, Kristina would be re-sentenced to life in prison with the possibility of parole.

The judge also recommended that she be immediately paroled due to her illness.

The decision on whether or not to set her free set off a firestorm of controversy in Kristina's own family and the state of Iowa.

"To give her her last few moments of joy and peace," Kristina's mother Denise Fetters said. "I think could be the best thing that she could receive."

But other family members weren't so keen on that idea.

"I just don't feel bad for Krissy for where she's at," Kristina's cousin, Shanna Sickles said. "She put herself there. She didn't give my Aunt Arlene the opportunity to die with her loved ones. Bottom line, if you get life in prison without the possibility of parole, it's life."

But Kristina also had her supporters in friend Jaimi Ross.

"I completely understand when people say things like 'Oh, a life for a life, she took a life, she should die in prison,'" Ross said. "That states more about where you're at in life, and not her, not me and not her family. I get that that's where your heart is and that's what you believe. Were not asking for her to have a second chance."

The parole board decided to release Kristina on a hospice-only basis. There was outcry from people who wanted her to stay in jail, stating that the prison only set her free to save on medical costs.

In the end, the bureaucracy mattered little as Kristina had already reached stage four with her cancer.

"No one can alter the past," Kristina's aunt Darcy Olson said. "It is what it is, this happened to our family and it's now time for my family to have closure. Kristina's impending death cannot be denied and while there have been negative comments, we believe, as the victims, our family has suffered enough and we ask the parole board to grant our request."

Darcy was the only family member aside from Kristina's mother that supported her during the trial and parole hearings.

"It's just so bitter sweet," Olson said. "This has been a 19-year old tragedy for my family. This will bring closure for my whole family and help us all cope just a little bit better with the situation."

"Everybody's like, well, she was a monster," Ross said. "She was evil. It would be so easy in this world if that were just the case. But that's not the way that it is. Not everybody that commits a crime...not everybody that's a sinner is evil or a monster. Her legacy, I hope, will challenge other people to see what they can do for kids. For teenagers. Before it gets to the point where they're in prison or needing to go before a judge for any reason."

The cancer would spread throughout her bones and spine. Kristina would live out her last days in pain.

"The screams I had to listen to last Sunday, no mother should ever have to hear in her life," Kristina's mother, Denise said.

Seven months into her release, Kristina would die at the age of thirty-four.

bonus:

Brittany Holberg was a twenty-three years old prostitute when she was convicted of murdering 80-year-old A.B. Towery Jr, stabbing him over sixty times.

The controversy surrounding the case centered around the relationship of Brittany and Towery prior to the killing. Brittany argued that Towery was a client who went into a rage when he found drugs on her person. He attacked her and she retaliated in self-defense.

Further investigation would reveal otherwise, however, as Brittany would use numerous household items in a brutal assault on the elderly man.

She fled the scene only to be caught at a McDonald's after police received a tip from a witness who saw her on "America's Most Wanted."

With her good looks and well-proportioned body, Brittany has remained in the spotlight as she was featured in a Maxim Magazine article as one of the "hottest women on death row".

Brittany still sits on death row today with her case being appealed on the numerous levels in the court system.

EARLY LIFE

Brittany was born on January 1, 1973, in Amarillo, Texas.

Accounts on Brittany's home life vary as she would manipulate according to the needs of her listener. To her probation officer, she informed them that her home life was "good" and that she "had everything that she ever wanted". She would often describe her mother as her best friend.

During other occasions, however, Brittany would paint a different story.

She would describe her parents as being "hippie-drugsters". Brittany would state that she was close to her mother but never knew her father, a heroin addict who was in and out of the Texas prison system. Her mother would later marry a man named John Schwartz with the couple marrying and divorcing four times.

They would drink heavily and openly smoke weed in front of the young Brittany who would be sexually assaulted by a babysitter at the age of five. When she was twelve, one of her aunts was murdered and according to Brittany "everything fell apart" at home. Her parents would leave her unattended as they indulged in pot and booze.

"They just stopped working," Brittany said. "They just let everything go."

She would be gang raped by two men who confronted her in an alley behind her home when she was thirteen.

Brittany would then spend the majority of her time living with her grandmother. By the age of sixteen, however, she would run away with her boyfriend Ward. The two would make it as far as California, get married, and have a young daughter named Mackenzie.

The union would not last long, however. Brittany would divorce Ward and move back to her native Amarillo. Ward would take Mackenzie and move to Tulsa, Oklahoma.

Brittany would state that she suffered a knee injury and would become addicted to pain medication during treatment. She would then graduate to harder drugs like cocaine.

In and out of rehab, Brittany's life spiraled out of control. She could manipulate with the best of them, however, and would escape from the Midland Halfway House with the help of a female counselor.

Brittany would hang out with the drug-using crowd and her own habits were out of control. To support her addiction, Brittany began working as a prostitute.

This would put her in harm's way on many an occasion as she would get gang-raped and beaten severely.

The assault would put her in the hospital but she would resume "tricking" when she was released.

"At that point in her life, Brittany was incorrigible," forensic psychologist Paula Orange said."Numerous people had reached to her and tried to help. She had extended family members trying to help.

Friends trying to help. Even church outreach workers. All to no avail. The drugs had taken root and she was dead set on manipulating everyone around her. Family, roommates, church members, doctors, dentists, and pharmacists would all fall victim to her schemes to get drugs."

By 1993, Brittany was a full-blown drug-addicted prostitute with the rap sheet to prove it. In April of that year, she would steal a gun from her step-father. She then passed over $1300 in "hot" checks and applied for several store credit cards using a fake name.

Brittany and one of her aunts would run a scam on dentists, lying to them about their pain levels in order to get prescription medication. When the prescription drugs ran out, she would return to street drugs like cocaine and heroin. Arrests would follow and Brittany would be charged in Hale County with drug possession, paraphernalia, and public intoxication.

Upon her release, Brittany would proceed to steal her mother's car and forge checks in her name. The prostitution continued unabated as well as she stole the wallet from one of her "tricks" who pressed charges.

While in jail for the theft, Brittany would be introduced to Ella Gibbs and Patricia Karnes who ran the ministry in the Randall County Jail. The women tried to get Brittany on the right track and introduce her to Christianity.

"I wanted to reassure Brittany that she is a valuable person, that her life has great potential, and that this is the mortal portion of an eternal life," Karnes said. " Brittany is an eternal being and through the many prayers from my [prayer] group [in Lubbock,] I have been led to come back into this child's life to support her here, to encourage her, to find her courage from the Holy Spirit within her, and to let her know that there is a human being mortal person who will stand beside her and see the good in her and support whatever God plans for the rest of your [sic] life."

A.B. TOWERY

Towery was by all accounts a nice man. His son would bristle at the idea that he was Brittany's "sugar daddy".

"Dad wasn't a dirty old man," his son said. "Dad was just trying to help somebody and look what he got, and now she's getting three meals a day and a warm place to sleep."

The defense would later bring up the fact that he once pulled a knife on his son Russell during a temper tantrum. Towery would have a history with prostitutes (according to court testimony). Connie Baker would be a prostitute from the 1980s to 1997 and stated that Towery was one of her clients. Baker would also claim Tower as a client but she also had a history of drug possession and auto theft. Diana Wheeler would also admit to being one of Towery's prostitutes in the years of 1994 and 1995. She had come to his home and he even went so far as to clean the stains off his Mel Mac dinnerware. But Wheeler also had a long criminal history like Baker, arrested for prostitution, criminal trespass and giving false identification to a police officer.

The controversy at the trial was if Brittany and Towery had an ongoing "sex-for-money" relationship.

This would be vigorously discounted by family members.

His daughter-in-law would come to the home and help with some housekeeping. His sons would also visit daily and never report any "ladies of the evening" coming to visit their father.

The picture just didn't fit.

Brittany stated she was sent to Towery's place by a fellow streetwalker who went by the moniker of "Green Eyes" but that it was later revealed that no such prostitute by that name existed. Brittany had lied like she had so many times before.

The two seemed to have met by chance.

COMING BACK FROM THE GROCERY STORE

November 13th, 1996 was another normal day for the 80-year old A.B Towery. He had just purchased groceries at an Albertson's store and was walking back to his apartment. As he entered the courtyard, he was approached by the 23-year old Brittany Holberg.

She asked to use his telephone and Towery consented. He wanted to help the sweet-voiced Brittany and didn't believe that she posed any kind of physical threat to him.

What he didn't know was that Brittany was coming down from a cocaine high and had not slept in ten days.

"Brittany could be persuasive," Orange said. "She was well-versed in how to charm people, she knew exactly what to say and do in terms of body language. She was like a trained actress. It didn't take much cajoling on her part to convince Towery to let her inside his home. He probably thought 'what's the big deal?'"

Once inside, Brittany would demand money from the elderly man but he refused. Brittany then attacked Towery, trying to strong arm the wallet out of his pocket. The struggle began in the living room. The two then pushed and pulled each other around a partition that separated the kitchen from the living room. They then returned to the living room. At some point, Towery tried to leave the apartment but Brittany pulled him back in. The evidence also indicated that the two paused during this 45-minute fight, catching their breath and nursing their wounds. Brittany would sustain minor stab wounds to her stomach and thigh.

"This was most likely a fight that had a lot of clutching and grabbing," Orange said. "There was less blood in the living room so the conjecture is that is where the fight started. There was blood near the door so that suggests that Towery was bleeding out and trying to escape for help. Remember, he was a slow-moving 80-year old man. Brittany was a young woman but she was fueled by cocaine. He's getting tired a lot faster than she will."

Eventually, Brittany gained the upper hand. She used various objects around the home to beat down Towery. She started with a cast iron frying pan, then a steam iron, a claw hammer, a fruit knife, a butcher knife and then two forks. Towery would fall to the floor, a bloody mess.

Brittany then took a lamp and shoved its base five inches down his throat which choked him to death.

Satisfied that he had finally killed Tower, Brittany removed her bloody clothes. She washed up in his bathroom then went to his closet to find some clothes that fit her.

Walking back to his dead body, Brittany retrieved the wallet out of Towery's pocket. She took out the $1400 dollars he had and dropped the now empty wallet onto his stomach.

Brittany casually walked out of the apartment and hitched a ride with a young couple. The couple dropped her off at a local crack house where Brittany paid them off with two $100 bills (which had blood stains on them). Inside the drug den, Brittany befriended the proprietor and changed clothes again. She then went to a local hotel with hundreds of dollars worth of cocaine and indulged.

TRIAL

Brittany's defense attorney, Catherine Brown Dodson, would argue that Holberg acted in self-defense when she killed Towery. Her primary argument was that Towery was far from an innocent, elderly man. He was, in fact, a drug abuser himself who became physically violent with Brittany when he found a crack pipe on her person. He then hit Brittany two times in the head when she turned her back to him. Brittany retaliated and ultimately put the lamp post in his mouth in an attempt to end the fight.

Brittany then fled as she believed that no one would believe her side of the story because she was both a prostitute and a drug addict.

While in jail, Brittany would try to coerce Katina Dixon, her cellmate to kill Vickie Marie Kirkpatrick who was the prosecution witness.

Towery's history with prostitutes would be brought up in court testimony. They would also mention incidents of violence with his ex-wife and children but jurors didn't believe the old man was in any type of shape to employ the service of a prostitute.

"My father didn't even like the word 'sex'", one of his sons said. "He was old-fashioned."

A psychiatrist would testify, however, that Brittany had battered wife syndrome, post-traumatic stress disorder, and cocaine addiction.

The jury did not take long to deliberate, finding Brittany to be a cunning, manipulative liar who committed one of the most brutal crimes in the history of Amarillo.

They would find her guilty and Brittany would be moved to death row at Gatesville, Texas.

"I can't even explain to you," Brittany said in a magazine interview. "What it's like to have someone say 'You are sentenced to die.' It's words. You feel helpless, numb. It's almost as if your emotions shut you down."

Brittany would spend her first few weeks in prison laying prone on her bed in a zombie-like state. Over time, she grew accepting of her situation. She knew she was going to die but made it a point to learn to take each day one step at a time.

Her inspiration for cleaning up her act came from the memory of her daughter Mackenzie.

"I cannot live," Brittany said. "And I cannot die, knowing that my child has to live with the horror that these people tried to say about me, the story of the crime, their depiction that I was a cold-blooded person."

Brittany states that she dedicates her days to reading, writing to family and working on her law appeals. She also is anti-death penalty advocate.

She would follow other Texas inmates who were now on death row and make appeals on their behalf, specifically that of Betty Lou Beets.

"I realized," Brittany said. "It doesn't matter whether I'm guilty or innocent, this has now become a very political thing... At this point, they're just killing to kill."

She complained that after a recent jail uprising, the treatment of death row inmates has worsened.

"You would not believe the treatment we are given," Brittany said. "Just two weeks ago, we were informed that not only would we be strip-searched for our one hour of recreation a day, but also when taken for a shower. So for the last two weeks, we have been stripped no less than six times a day. This is every day, sometimes at times like 2:30-3 a.m., and we never leave the building or our cells for that matter."

As of this writing, Brittany's stay of execution has been appealed and appealed for the past eighteen years.

Her attorneys would exhaust the appeal process in the state system but it is now in the federal courts.

Her case, however, has been costing taxpayers "conservatively to be at least $400,000" according to county criminal attorney James Farren. In the future, he has decided to forgo seeking the death penalty in capital cases.

Farren continues to favor a death penalty but only under certain circumstances like "a guy walks into a day care center and kills the children or if someone kills a police officer or a firefighter in the line of duty."

Farren predicted that Brittany would remain on death row for another five years at least. "They can go through the U.S District Court in Amarillo, then it can go to the Fifth U.S Circuit Court and the U.S. Supreme Court. Then from there it can go back to the U.S. District."

But the appeals can come to a halt if the district judge refuses to hear it again.

"If the Supreme Court says 'no'," Farren said. "That's when the district judge can feel safe in stopping this process."

The entire process has been an infuriating one for the Towery family. His son both rages and mourns about what happened to his father.

"She tried to apologize to us during the trial," Russel Towery said. " I got up and walked out. I'm sure other families are going through the same things I'm going through. It's been almost 19 years ... people forget."

"I don't want to die before she does. I want to stand there as she's kicking and screaming going to the death gurney. I want her to think about what my dad went through when she didn't even know his name," he said. "She thinks that because she said she was sorry, that everything's all right. ... she is evil and needs to be destroyed."

KILLER TEEN NIKKI REYNOLDS

SAMANTHA REED

It is not often that stories appear where we find the perpetrators of violence being children and the victims being parents. Although, scattered throughout history it has been seen that children can be capable of shocking amounts of violence, and many, assuming their innocent nature, fall victim to them. In Coral Springs, Florida in 1997 one such story took place. And still the actions of the evening resonate throughout the community.

In The Beginning

Born in 1979 to a mother that didn't want her, Jacquiline "Nikki" Reynolds was adopted by Robert and Billie Jean Reynolds three months after her birth. The Reynolds were a loving, Christian family from Coral Springs, Florida and they were delighted to welcome their new daughter into their lives.

There was nothing that they wouldn't do for Nikki. Robert Reynolds worked for the Department of Transportation and Billie Jean was an administrative assistant at RJ Reynolds. They had a quiet home and they were devoted to making their daughter happy.

Nikki was a good child. She was devoted to the church, like her parents, and she loved her parents deeply. She would go to the mall with her mother or watch baseball games with her father. She could never spend too much time with them. The Reynolds did everything to ensure that Nikki was being raised in a loving and non-judgmental environment.

Friends and family would agree that the environment was loving, but the Reynolds gave Nikki everything she wanted. She was pampered, she was spoiled, and in the end, she was a bit of a brat. Sometimes the best intentions can have the worst consequences.

Still, Nikki, as she got older, became a good student and didn't act out. She achieved good grades in school and went out of her way to become involved in extra curricular activities. She also stayed heavily involved with the church alongside her parents.

By all appearances, Nikki was the perfect child. She was the child that most parents dream of having and Robert and Billie Jean were delighted with her. But children grow up, despite anything that their parents try to do to stop it, and Nikki was no exception. And not all children grow up in a manner that their parents can be proud of.

The Beginning of the End

Nikki went from being the model child to what most people would call a 'troubled teen'. It didn't start in the way one would expect, with failing grades and a lack of interest in school. It started with a lie, and one that shocked family and friends in the disturbing nature of it.

In 1996, sixteen-year-old Nikki came home from school and claimed that she had been assaulted after getting off of the school bus. Naturally her parents were shocked and appalled to hear that this had happened to her. They immediately called the police to handle the situation officially. Nikki claimed she had been attacked by someone she knew, at first. But when questioned by the police her story quickly changed.

She went on to say that she didn't know her attacker and then that the attack hadn't happened at all. She hadn't been raped. She'd made the whole story up.

Now why would a sixteen-year-old, devote Christian girl make up a story about being raped? Why would she go to the extreme of telling her parents and getting the police involved if it was just a story?

It turns out that Nikki hadn't been raped. Rather she was in a relationship, the first one of a sexual nature in her lifetime, and she was terrified to tell her parents about it. She was worried about what they would think about their daughter sacrificing her morals and her principles just to have a boyfriend. But Carlos Infante was her entire world. The sixteen-year-old classmate was consuming her life focus to the point that she hadn't hesitated to throw caution to the wind.

And when the thought of telling her parents about what was going on had come up, in her mind, fabricating a rape story had seemed like a better idea. Nikki was also concerned that she might be pregnant, a worry that was quickly put to rest, but it also influenced her decision to pursue the rape narrative.

Billie Jean was extremely unhappy with Nikki, potentially for the first time during her parenting of the girl. She didn't like the fact that Nikki had a boyfriend. She didn't like the fact that she'd sacrificed her principles and morals, the beliefs that they thought they'd instilled into her all for some boy. They believed that they'd raised a good, Christian girl and for the first time they were starting to question that belief.

Bille Jean and Robert disliked the idea of Nikki having a boyfriend, it didn't particularly matter who he was. They viewed it as a step down for her. They saw it as a complete abandonment of her belief system, something they had strived to instill in her over the course of her entire life. She was sacrificing everything in order to be with this boy, from their point of view. She was losing herself in him. And Billie Jean and Robert wanted to help get Nikki back on a clear path, on a Christian path.

So, they insisted that she spend less time with Carlos and more time with the church. They hoped that in doing so she would see her wrongdoings and find her true self again. They hoped that in spending more time with the church that she would become closer to the family again and forget about Carlos.

Billie Jean believed that Nikki needed to spend more time with a better group of people, a Christian group of people. She hoped that if Nikki spent time around other good, Christian kids that she would find her way again, that she would find a better crowd. And Billie Jean was willing to go to great lengths to ensure that her daughter found a path that fit with the beliefs and morals of the family.

But sometimes the child, no matter how much they push, cannot realize the hopes and dreams of parents. And sometimes, despite all efforts, things still go wrong.

Rebellion Continues

Teenage rebellion can be a strong force, however, and the more that Billie Jean pushed Nikki to go to church the more she resisted. Nikki said, "I knew that the way I was living was not right in God's eyes, but I did not want to hear all of that." She was too engulfed in her life with Carlos. He was quickly becoming her entire world and nothing else mattered to her. Not her parents, and certainly not her church.

The rebellion was extending into her school life. Nikki, who had once been a good student with marks that her parents could be proud of was now beginning to skip class. Her grades were beginning to fall as a result and she was no longer the academic force that she was before.

It was to the point that Billie Jean and Robert barely recognized the girl that they had raised anymore. Who was this young woman living in their house? She reflected none of the morals and principles they had raised her to uphold. She wouldn't listen to them. She opposed them at every turn. They began to wonder what had happened to their daughter Nikki. Where had she gone?

Nikki went from a happy-go-lucky child that was a pleasure to be around, a child who was soft spoken and loved to go to church to a girl no one could recognize. She wore dark clothes, she changed her music, she changed her bedroom to dark colours – she became the opposite of herself. It was hard to tell if this was simply teenage rebellion or something more going on. Was this all because of Carlos or was there some deeper problem at play?

She slept a lot, more than any teenager should and she isolated herself from her family. Gone were the days of ice cream and base ball games. She no longer went on trips to the mall with her mother. She no longer went to church with her family. She became disinterested in many things that used to hold her attention, things that used to captivate her. Her whole world now revolved around Carlos.

It was her first sexual relationship with anyone in her life and it had reached the point of obsession. She filled her diary with everything to do with Carlos. Her room was plastered with photos of him. Her every waking moment revolved around him. There was an unnatural intensity to her emotions towards him, an unhealthy intensity. And it was quickly becoming evident that this was a problem.

Naturally, Billie Jean and Robert were very concerned about their daughter's current mental state. She was not herself, and the only thing they could blame was Carlos as he was the only changing factor in her life. It seemed that he was a negative influence on Nikki in many ways. He didn't make good grades as a student, and now her grades were plummeting as well.

Billie Jean was also worried that he was coming over every day, potentially when they were at work. They had no way to confirm this, but she didn't like the idea that he was at the house alone with her while they were at work. It didn't sit well with her.

So Billie Jean put her foot down, perhaps for the first time in her experience as a parent. She began to tell Nikki no, especially when it came to Carlos. And Nikki handled it with the maturity level of a toddler as opposed to that of a teenager. Nikki threw awful tantrums. Billie Jean and Nikki would engage in screaming matches in the house that would result in slammed doors. The result was very wearing on Billie Jean. She found herself screaming at Nikki almost all of the time. This was not what she wanted her life as a mother to be. This was not the girl she had raised. She needed to do something about this, but she was at a loss as to what the solution could be.

And despite the screaming matches and the orders to stay away, Nikki still kept seeing Carlos. It seemed that nothing could keep her from Carlos. She would sneak out at night when everyone was asleep to see him and it didn't matter what the consequences were.

Billie Jean's frustration escalated to the point that one day she confided in a friend saying "Don't be surprised if one day you come home and there's police cars and fire trucks up and down the street 'cause one of us, it'll be me or Nikki, but one of us will be gone."

Billie Jean's prediction would prove to hit a little too close to home in the coming days. And the aftermath would shock everyone.

Intervention

It was May 14, 1997 when the school counselor contacted Billie Jean to tell her that there was trouble with Nikki and Carlos. She asked that Billie Jean come in and speak with her in person and that Billie Jean, Robert, and Nikki come in for a full meeting the next day. Upon visiting the high school, the counselor told Billie Jean that Nikki and Carlos had more than just the usual high school relationship issues to deal with.

That day Nikki had told the counselor that she was pregnant with Carlos' baby. This had naturally prompted the counselor to contact Billie Jean immediately about the issue. Billie Jean, having already dealt with Nikki's questionable honesty with the previous rape accusation, was hesitant to believe the pregnancy claim. She was fairly certain that this was another one of Nikki's schemes, but there was a sure way to determine its legitimacy.

So she took Nikki to the drug store to find out what was what.

The results of the pregnancy test were negative. That didn't mean Billie Jean was any less pleased with her daughter. Nikki called Carlos with the news. And despite having a counseling meeting the next day Billie Jean decided to seek guidance from a higher power. She dragged Nikki away from the phone and took Nikki to see the church counselor.

Nikki spoke with her pastor as they waited to see the counselor. He was supportive as he talked to her about her boyfriend problems and offered her guidance. Their conversation with the counselor did not have the same supportive tone. The counselor spent the session telling Nikki that her mother did not deserve the behaviour she was displaying. She raised her voice and yelled at Nikki. This didn't go over very well.

Nikki removed herself from the office and from the church. She wanted nothing more to do with the impromptu counseling session. And as she stood in the parking lot of the church she even debated removing herself from the family by running away. But she didn't run away, however. Instead, she took a higher ground, something that hadn't been seen from her in almost a year. She went back into the counselor's office and apologized to her mother. And she finished the session with the counselor before returning home with her mother.

Billie Jean believed that they had made a step in the right direction. She would be the one to learn how wrong she was about that fact.

Confusion and Confessions

It was barely an hour after their visit to the counselor on May 14, 1997 that the call came in to 911. At 7:07pm Nikki Reynolds' panicked voice came over the phone saying "I stabbed her repeatedly in the back. There's blood all over her and all over the floor and everything."

Police were at her house in minutes and the scene that they witnessed was one that would stay with some of the officers for years after. When police arrived they found Nikki waiting on her doorstep. One of the officers who responded indicated that "She had blood all over, blood on her legs, blood on her face."

Nikki was placed in the back of the police car and left to wait while the police went to investigate. A tape recorder was left on with her in the police car so that anything that was said while she was alone was recorded and on file. It recorded her praying that her mother was still be alive and saying that she had learned her lesson. She was asking God to forgive her and for her mother to please still be alive.

Her mother was brought out of the house on a stretcher by the EMTs and she was still alive at the time that she left the house. However, Billie Jean was pronounced dead at the hospital at 8:10pm after suffering from 13 stab wounds.

Nikki was taken to the police department immediately. Robert came home from work to find the house in a state of chaos, surrounded by police cars and police tape. He hadn't yet been informed of the situation that had come to pass behind the front doors of his home. He broke down at the news that his wife was gone and that his daughter was responsible. The shock of it was something that he couldn't quite comprehend.

The scene inside the house was gruesome and shocking to police investigators. It depicted Billie Jean's terrible, drawn out death as she fought to get away from her daughter. But there was no escape for her as she was stabbed repeatedly until she finally lay immobile on the floor.

The police found the kitchen knife that had been used as the murder weapon in the sink and it still had blood on it. They also found evidence that someone, likely Nikki, had attempted to clean up the scene using towels and dishcloths. The blood soaked pieces of cloth were scattered about the kitchen unable to handle the sheer amount of blood that had resulted from the incident.

While the police officers worked diligently at the crime seen the detectives questioned Nikki about the murder. And it didn't take too much effort to get her to talk.

"I didn't have any intentions of lying." Nikki said. "I didn't have any secrets. I wanted to get it out." She felt almost compelled to tell the story of what had happened. She needed to let them know.

"It was simple, all I had to ask her was what happened today and just started chatting. She went through the whole story from a to b," said the detective who interviewed Nikki.

The story that was told by Nikki revolved heavily around Carlos Infante, the infamous boyfriend. Nikki had used her fake pregnancy to keep Carlos in a relationship with her when he wanted to leave, fearing what would happen if he left. When she had found out she was not pregnant, for sure, she called him to give the news. Carlos indicated that he wanted nothing to do with her and all of her lies. He'd had enough. Billie Jean had even got on the phone with Carlos and apologized for all of the drama that he'd had to endure at the hands of her daughter.

Nikki had decided then and there that someone would die that day. She even took a handful of aspirin before going to the counseling meeting with her mother at the church. She was certain that she could overdose on it. She was certain that it would be her that would die.

However, when the overdose failed her thoughts went from suicide to homicide rather quickly. But the intended victim had not been her mother.

Her plan had been to get a hold of Carlos the next day and kill him. She figured she could catch him after first hour and slash his throat if she snuck up behind him. She believed that if she couldn't have him then no one should be allowed to have him. He belonged to her essentially.

However, the one obstacle in her plan to kill Carlos was the meeting they had with the guidance counselor the next day. Nikki was unsure whether she would be sent home after the meeting or not. In order to kill Carlos she would have to skip the guidance meeting. So, in order to accomplish this, she figured she would have to kill her parents as well. She would just wait until they were sleeping and then simply slash their throats. Then they could no longer stand in her way.

A real obstacle came into this metaphorical plan when her father left for church after dinner that night alone and her mother stayed home. This was very out of character for them. Nikki also stayed home as her mother told her she was grounded for the rest of the evening. She was instructed to clean the dishes after dinner.

Nikki decided that she would just roll with this change. She believed, since she was now home alone with her mother, that it would be much easier to kill her mother now, clean up the mess, and then wait until her father returned. She could then kill him and do the same. Finally, she could drive herself to school in the morning, wait for

Carlos, and kill him after first hour just like she had planned. It would work out perfectly.

Logical thought was gone at this point in time. Nikki was acting strictly on whatever thoughts came to her mind and they were frantic, desperate. Still, she waited for her opportunity to arrive. She waited for her moment when she could kill her mother.

Opportunity came while she was cleaning up in the kitchen and Billie Jean was working at her computer. Nikki took a kitchen knife, paused for a moment to check the blade for its sharpness, and then slowly approached her mother. She hesitated now that she had the knife in hand. She wasn't sure what it would feel like to slash someone's throat.

When she finally got up the nerve to come up behind her mother and attempt to cut her throat it didn't slash it, it only cut it. Billie Jean jumped up in surprise and darted towards the laundry room. She screamed, "No, Nikki, no."

"I told her I had to kill her because I can't live without Carlos," Nikki explained to police in her interview.

Nikki kept stabbing her because she wanted to put her out of her misery, she claims. She didn't want her mother to suffering any longer. And in her last moments, Billie Jean still offered her daughter forgiveness for killing her.

Nikki spent one night in the hospital because of her claim of ingesting a large amount of Aspirin. After that she was turned over to the county jail where she was formally booked on a charge of First Degree Murder.

The First Trial
The first trial for Nikki Reynolds lasted from April 14, 1999 – May 3, 1999.

If convicted, Nikki faced life in prison after spending two years in a Juvenile Detention Centre. The prosecution built their case around Nikki's obsession with Carlos Infante, making sure to indicate that he was not at fault in any way and rather he was also one of the three listed on Nikki's kill list.

The defence opted to take an insanity plea route, rather than try to dispute the charge that Nikki had committed the murder – something she had confessed to multiple times. This defence fell flat. The criterion for an insanity plea is very strict. The accused has to suffer from a serious mental illness and the accused has to be unaware that what they are doing is wrong or has consequences.

The psychologist that testified for the prosecution indicated that Nikki was well aware of what she was doing, and rather that she was just a confused girl. The defence tried to argue that Nikki suffered from Borderline Personality disorder. They claimed that individuals suffering from this disorder could idolize the individuals they are with and then suddenly snap, and become violent. Which is very similar to Nikki's reaction after Carlos indicated he wanted nothing to do with her. They also claimed that the Aspirin played a part as Aspirin can cause metabolic imbalances and psychosis upon overdoes.

Regardless of the claims on either side, the jury was hung and the trial ended in a mistrial.

The Second Trial
Second trail for Nikki Reynolds began on Sept 1, 1999.

Similar to the first, the prosecution brought a series of psychologists to the stand to prove that, while not a rational act, Nikki was not insane. The prosecution also claimed that her mother's death was premeditated.

The defence countered that Nikki was mentally ill and called experts to speak to Nikki's sanity. The defence also brought forward Nikki's biological mother to testify. The birth mother had a long history of mental illness and family violence. The defence argued that it was the anxiety over losing Carlos that pushed Nikki over the edge and brought her mental illness to the surface.

After much deliberation, Nikki Reynolds was found guilty of Second Degree Murder at the end of the trial.

At the sentencing hearing on January 7, 2000 Nikki's biological mother made a plea to include treatment as a part of Nikki's sentence. She believed that her daughter needed help, much like she had needed help in her lifetime.

Nikki also addressed the court, pleading with the judge to sentence her to a psychiatric facility instead of prison. She truly believed that there had been something wrong that day, if not insanity, than something else. She believed that she needed help. She bore no ill will towards her family. She hated none of them. She had never hated them and still didn't.

However, the judge believed that the wrongness of what she had done to outweigh all else. He gave her the maximum sentence under Florida law, 34 years in prison. She was resentenced to 21 years and 8 months on April 4, 2001 due to a change in sentencing laws in the state of Florida.

In the end Robert Reynolds remarried in 1998 and has had no contact with his daughter since she was sent to prison on January 2000.

And Nikki was incarcerated at the Gadsden Correctional Facility in Quincy, Florida. She was eligible for parole in 2015 and was released.

Milton Keynes UK
Ingram Content Group UK Ltd.
UKHW051914300624
444825UK00001B/30

9 798224 165186